ENGLISH LITERATURE AND SOCIETY IN THE EIGHTEENTH CENTURY

ENGLISH LITERATURE AND SOCIETY IN THE EIGHTEENTH CENTURY

FORD LECTURES, 1903

By LESLIE STEPHEN

LONDON
DUCKWORTH and CO.
3 HENRIETTA STREET, W.C.
1904

Edinburgh : T. and A. Constable, Printers to His Majesty

TO HERBERT FISHER

NEW COLLEGE, OXFORD

MY DEAR HERBERT,—I had prepared these Lectures for delivery, when a serious breakdown of health made it utterly impossible for me to appear in person. The University was then good enough to allow me to employ a deputy; and you kindly undertook to read the Lectures for me. I have every reason to believe that they lost nothing by the change.

I need only explain that, although they had to be read in six sections, and are here divided into five chapters, no other change worth noticing has been made. Other changes probably ought to have been made, but my health has been unequal to the task of serious correction. The publication has been delayed from the same cause.

Meanwhile, I wish to express my gratitude for your services. I doubt, too, whether I should have ventured to republish them, had it not been for your assertion that they have some interest. I would adopt the good old form of dedicating them to you, were it not that I can find no precedent for a dedication by an uncle to a nephew—uncles having, I fancy, certain opinions as to the light in which they are generally regarded by nephews. I will not say what that is, nor mention another reason which has its weight. I will only say that, though this is not a dedication, it is meant to express a very warm sense of gratitude due to you upon many grounds. —Your affectionate

LESLIE STEPHEN.

November 1903.

PUBLISHERS' NOTE

Owing to the ill-health of Sir Leslie Stephen the proofs have been passed for press by Mr. H. Fisher, Fellow of New College, who read the Lectures at Oxford on behalf of the Author.

ENGLISH LITERATURE AND SOCIETY IN THE EIGHTEENTH CENTURY

I

When I was honoured by the invitation to deliver this course of lectures, I did not accept without some hesitation. I am not qualified to speak with authority upon such subjects as have been treated by my predecessors—the course of political events or the growth of legal institutions. My attention has been chiefly paid to the history of literature, and it might be doubtful whether that study is properly included in the phrase 'historical.' Yet literature expresses men's thoughts and passions, which have, after all, a considerable influence upon their lives. The writer of a people's songs, as we are told, may even have a more powerful influence than the maker of their laws. He certainly reveals more directly the true springs of popular action. The truth has been admitted by many historians who are too much overwhelmed by state papers to find space for any extended application of the method. No one, I think, has shown more clearly how much light could be derived from this source than your Oxford historian J. R. Green, in some brilliant passages of his fascinating book. Moreover, if I may venture to speak of myself, my own interest in literature has always been closely connected with its philosophical and social significance. Literature may of course be studied simply for its own intrinsic merits. But it may also be regarded as one manifestation of what is called 'the spirit of the age.' I have, too, been much impressed by a further conclusion. No one doubts that the speculative movement affects the social and political—I think that less attention has been given to the reciprocal influence. The philosophy of a period is often treated as though it were the product of impartial and abstract investigation — something worked out by the great thinker in his study and developed by simple logical deductions from the positions established by his predecessors. To my mind, though I cannot now dwell upon the point, the philosophy of an age is in itself determined to a very great extent by the social position. It gives the solutions of the problems forced upon the reasoner by the practical conditions of his time. To understand why certain ideas become current, we have to consider not merely the ostensible logic but all the motives which led men to investigate the most pressing difficulties suggested by the social development. Obvious principles are always ready, like germs, to come to life when the congenial soil is provided. And what is true of the philosophy is equally, and perhaps more conspicuously, true of the artistic and literary embodiment of the dominant ideas which are correlated with the social movement.

A recognition of the general principle is implied in the change which has come over the methods of criticism. It has more and more adopted the historical attitude. Critics in an earlier day conceived their function to be judicial. They were administering a fixed code of laws applicable in all times and places. The true canons for dramatic or epic poetry, they held, had been laid down once for all by Aristotle or his commentators; and the duty of the critic was to consider whether the author had infringed or conformed to the established rules, and to pass sentence accordingly. I will not say that the modern critic has abandoned altogether that conception of his duty. He seems to me not infrequently to place himself on the judgment-seat with a touch of his old confidence, and to sentence poor authors with sufficient airs of infallibility. Sometimes, indeed, the reflection that he is representing not an invariable tradition but the last new æsthetic doctrine, seems even to give additional keenness to his opinions and to suggest no doubts of his infallibility. And yet there is a change in his position. He admits, or at any rate is logically bound to admit, the code which he administers requires modification in different times and places. The old critic spoke like the organ of an infallible Church, regarding all forms of art except his own as simply heretical. The modern critic speaks like the liberal theologian, who sees in heretical and heathen creeds an approximation to the truth, and admits that they may have a relative value, and even be the best fitted for the existing conditions. There are, undoubtedly, some principles of universal application; and the old critics often expounded them with admirable common-sense and force. But like general tenets of morality, they are apt to be commonplaces, whose specific application requires knowledge of concrete facts. When the critics assumed that the forms familiar to themselves were the only possible embodiments of those principles, and condemned all others as barbarous, they were led to pass judgments, such, for example, as Voltaire's view of Dante and Shakespeare, which strike us as strangely crude and unappreciative. The change in this, as in other departments of thought, means again that criticism, as Professor Courthope has said, must become thoroughly inductive. We must start from experience. We must begin by asking impartially what pleased men, and then inquire why it pleased them. We must not decide dogmatically that it ought to have pleased or displeased on the simple ground that it is or is not congenial to ourselves. As historical methods extend, the same change takes place in regard to political or economical or religious, as well as in regard to literary investigations. We can then become catholic enough to appreciate varying forms; and recognise that each has its own rules, right under certain conditions and appropriate within the given sphere. The great empire of literature, we may say, has many provinces. There is a 'law of nature' deducible from universal principles of reason which is applicable throughout, and enforces what may be called the cardinal virtues common to all forms of human expression. But subordinate to this, there is also a municipal law, varying in every province and determining the particular systems which are applicable to the different state of things existing in each region.

This method, again, when carried out, implies the necessary connection between the social and literary departments of history. The adequate criticism must be rooted in history. In some sense I am ready to admit that all criticism is a nuisance and a parasitic growth upon literature. The most fruitful reading is that in which we are submitting to a teacher and asking no questions as to the secret of his influence. Bunyan had no knowledge of the 'higher criticism'; he read into the Bible a great many dogmas which were not there, and accepted rather questionable historical data. But perhaps he felt some essential characteristics of the book more thoroughly than far more cultivated people. No critic can instil into a reader that spontaneous sympathy with the thoughts and emotions incarnated in the great masterpieces without which all reading is cold and valueless. In spite of all differences of dialect and costume, the great men can place themselves in spiritual contact with men of most distant races and periods. Art, we are told, is immortal. In other words, is unprogressive. The great imaginative creations have not been superseded. We go to the last new authorities for our science and our history, but the essential thoughts and emotions of human beings were incarnated long ago with unsurpassable clearness. When FitzGerald published his *Omar Khayyām*, readers were surprised to find that an ancient Persian had given utterance to thoughts which we considered to be characteristic of our own day. They had no call to be surprised. The writer of the Book of Job had long before given the most forcible expression to thought which still moves our deepest feelings; and Greek poets had created unsurpassable utterance for moods common to all men in all ages.

> 'Still green with bays each ancient altar stands
> Above the reach of sacrilegious hands,'

as Pope puts it; and when one remembers how through all the centuries the masters of thought and expression have appealed to men who knew nothing of criticism, higher or lower, one is tempted to doubt whether the critic be not an altogether superfluous phenomenon.

The critic, however, has become a necessity; and has, I fancy, his justification in his own sphere. Every great writer may be regarded in various aspects. He is, of course, an individual, and the critic may endeavour to give a psychological analysis of him; and to describe his intellectual and moral constitution and detect the secrets of his permanent influence without reference to the particular time and place of his appearance. That is an interesting problem when the materials are accessible. But every man is also an organ of the society in which he has been brought up. The material upon which he works is the whole complex of conceptions, religious, imaginative and ethical, which forms his mental atmosphere. That suggests problems for the historian of philosophy. He is also dependent upon what in modern phrase we call his 'environment'—the social structure of which he forms a part, and which gives a special direction to his passions and aspirations. That suggests problems for the historian of political and social institutions. Fully to appreciate any great writer, therefore, it is necessary to distinguish between the characteristics due to the individual with certain idiosyncrasies and the characteristics due to his special modification by the existing stage of social and intellectual development. In the earliest period the discrimination is impossible. Nobody, I suppose, not even if he be Provost of Oriel, can tell us much of the personal characteristics of the author—if there was an author—of the *Iliad*. He must remain for us a typical Greek of the heroic age; though even so, the attempt to realise the corresponding state of society may be of high value to an appreciation of the poetry. In later times we suffer from the opposite difficulty. Our descendants will be able to see the general characteristics of the Victorian age better than we, who unconsciously accept our own peculiarities, like the air we breathe, as mere matters of course. Meanwhile a Tennyson and a Browning strike us less as the organs of a society than by the idiosyncrasies which belong to them as individuals. But in the normal case, the relation of the two studies is obvious. Dante, for example, is profoundly interesting to the psychologist, considered simply as a human being. We are then interested by the astonishing imaginative intensity and intellectual power and the vivid personality of the man who still lives for us as he lived in the Italy of six centuries ago. But as all competent critics tell us, the *Divina Commedia* also reveals in the completest way the essential spirit of the Middle Ages. The two studies reciprocally enlighten each other. We know Dante and understand his position the more thoroughly as we know better the history of the political and ecclesiastical struggles in which he took part, and the philosophical doctrines which he accepted and interpreted; and conversely, we understand the period the better when we see how its beliefs and passions affected a man of abnormal genius and marked idiosyncrasy of character. The historical revelation is the more complete, precisely because Dante was not a commonplace or average person but a man of unique force, mental and moral. The remark may suggest what is the special value of the literary criticism or its bearing upon history. We may learn from many sources what was the current mythology of the day; and how ordinary people believed in devils and in a material hell lying just beneath our feet. The vision probably strikes us as repulsive and simply preposterous. If we proceed to ask what it meant and why it had so powerful a hold upon the men of the day, we may perhaps be innocent enough to apply to the accepted philosophers, especially to Aquinas, whose thoughts had been so thoroughly assimilated by the poet. No doubt that may suggest very interesting inquiries for the metaphysician ; but we should find not only that the philosophy is very tough and very obsolete, and therefore very wearisome for any but the strongest intellectual appetites, but also that it does not really answer our question. The philosopher does not give us the reasons which determine men to believe, but the official justification of their beliefs which has been elaborated by the most acute and laborious dialecticians. The inquiry shows how a philosophical system can be hooked on to an imaginative conception of the universe ; but it does not give the cause of the belief, only the way in which it can be more or less favourably combined with abstract logical principles. The great poet unconsciously reveals something more than the metaphysician. His poetry does not decay with the philosophy which it took for granted. We do not ask whether his reasoning be sound or false, but whether the vision be sublime or repulsive. It may be a little of both ; but at any rate it is undeniably fascinating. That, I take it, is because the imagery which he creates may still be a symbol of thoughts and emotions which are as interesting now as they were six hundred years ago. This man of first-rate power shows us, therefore, what was the real charm of the accepted beliefs for him, and less consciously for others. He had no doubt that their truth could be proved by syllogising: but they really laid so powerful a grasp upon him because they could be made to express the hopes and fears, the loves and hatreds, the moral and political convictions which were dearest to him. When we see how the system could be turned to account by the most powerful imagination, we can understand better what it really meant for the commonplace and ignorant monks who accepted it as a mere matter of course. We begin to see what were the great forces really at work below the surface ; and the issues which were being blindly worked out by the dumb agents who were quite unable to recognise their nature. If, in short, we wish to discover the secret of the great ecclesiastical and political struggles of the day, we should turn, not to the men in whose minds beliefs lie inert and instinctive, nor to the ostensible dialectics of the ostensible apologists and assailants, but to the great poet who shows how they were associated with the strongest passions and the most vehement convictions.

We may hold that the historian should confine himself to giving a record of the objective facts, which can be fully given in dates, statistics, and phenomena seen from outside. But if we allow ourselves to contemplate a philosophical history, which shall deal with the causes of events and aim at exhibiting the evolution of human society —and perhaps I ought to apologise for even suggesting that such an ideal could ever be realised—we should also see that the history of literature would be a subordinate element of the whole structure. The political, social, ecclesiastical, and economical factors, and their complex actions and reactions, would all have to be taken into account, the literary historian would be concerned with the ideas which find utterance through the poet and philosopher, and with the constitution of the class which at any time forms the literary organ of the society. The critic who deals with the individual work would find such knowledge necessary to a full appreciation of his subject; and, conversely, the appreciation would in some degree help the labourer in other departments of history to understand the nature of the forces which are governing the social development. However far we may be from such a consummation, and reluctant to indulge in the magniloquent language which it suggests, I imagine that a literary history is so far satisfactory as it takes the facts into consideration and regards literature, in the perhaps too pretentious phrase, as a particular function of the whole social organism. But I gladly descend from such lofty speculations to come to a few relevant details; and especially, to notice some of the obvious limitations which have in any case to be accepted.

And in the first place, when we try to be philosophical, we have a difficulty which besets us in political history. How much influence is to be attributed to the individual? Carlyle used to tell us in my youth that everything was due to the hero; that the whole course of human history depended upon your Cromwell or Frederick. Our scientific teachers are inclined to reply that no single person had much importance, and that an ideal history could omit all names of individuals. If, for example, Napoleon had been killed at the siege of Toulon, the only difference would have been that the dictator would have been called say

Moreau. Possibly, but I cannot see that we can argue in the same way in literature. I see no reason to suppose that if Shakespeare had died prematurely, anybody else would have written *Hamlet.* There was, it is true, a butcher's boy at Stratford, who was thought by his townsmen to have been as clever a fellow as Shakespeare. We shall never know what we have lost by his premature death, and we certainly cannot argue that if Shakespeare had died, the butcher would have lived. It makes one tremble, says an ingenious critic, to reflect that Shakespeare and Cervantes were both liable to the measles at the same time. As we know they escaped, we need not make ourselves unhappy about the might-have-been; but the remark suggests how much the literary glory of any period depends upon one or two great names. Omit Cervantes and Shakespeare and Molière from Spanish, English, and French literature, and what a collapse of glory would follow! Had Shakespeare died, it is conceivable perhaps that some of the hyperboles which have been lavished upon him would have been bestowed on Marlowe and Ben Jonson. But, on the whole, I fancy that the minor lights of the Elizabethan drama have owed more to their contemporary than he owed to them; and that, if this central sun had been extinguished, the whole galaxy would have remained in comparative obscurity. Now, as we are utterly unable to say what are the conditions which produce a genius, or to point to any automatic machinery which could replace him in case of accident, we must agree that this is an element in the problem which is altogether beyond scientific investigation. The literary historian must be content with a humble position. Still, the Elizabethan stage would have existed had Shakespeare never written; and, moreover, its main outline would have been the same. If any man ever imitated and gave full utterance to the characteristic ideas of his contemporaries it was certainly Shakespeare; and nobody ever accepted more thoroughly the form of art which they worked out. So far, therefore, as the general conditions of the time led to the elaboration of this particular genus, we may study them independently and assign certain general causes. What Shakespeare did was to show more fully the way in which that form could be turned to account; and, without him, it would have been a far less interesting phenomenon. Even the greatest man has to live in his own century.

The deepest thinker is not really—though we often use the phrase—in advance of his day so much as in the line along which advance takes place. The greatest poet does not write for a future generation in the sense of not writing for his own; it is only that in giving the fullest utterance to its thoughts and showing the deepest insight into their significance, he is therefore the most perfect type of its general mental attitude, and his work is an embodiment of the thoughts which are common to men of all generations.

When the critic began to perceive that many forms of art might be equally legitimate under different conditions, his first proceeding was to classify them in different schools. English poets, for example, were arranged by Pope and Gray as followers of Chaucer, Spenser, Donne, Dryden, and so forth; and, in later days, we have such literary genera as are indicated by the names classic and romantic or realist and idealist, covering characteristic tendencies of the various historical groups. The fact that literary productions fall into schools is of course obvious, and suggests the problem as to the cause of their rise and decline. Bagehot treats the question in his *Physics and Politics*. Why, he asks, did there arise a special literary school in the reign of Queen Anne—'a marked variety of human expression, producing what was then written and peculiar to it'? Some eminent writer, he replies, gets a start by a style congenial to the minds around him. Steele, a rough, vigorous, forward man, struck out the periodical essay; Addison, a wise, meditative man, improved and carried it to perfection. An unconscious mimicry is always producing countless echoes of an original writer. That, I take it, is undeniably true. Nobody can doubt that all authors are in some degree echoes, and that a vast majority are never anything else. But it does not answer why a particular form should be fruitful of echoes or, in Bagehot's words, be 'more congenial to the minds around.' Why did the *Spectator* suit one generation and the *Rambler* its successors? Are we incapable of giving any answer? Are changes in literary fashions enveloped in the same inscrutable mystery as changes in ladies' dresses? It is, and no doubt always will be, impossible to say why at one period garments should spread over a hoop and at another cling to the limbs. Is it equally impossible to say why the fashion of Pope should have been succeeded by the fashion of Wordsworth and

Coleridge? If we were prepared to admit the doctrine of which I have spoken—the supreme importance of the individual—that would of course be all that could be said. Shakespeare's successors are explained as imitators of Shakespeare, and Shakespeare is explained by his 'genius' or, in other words, is inexplicable. If, on the other hand, Shakespeare's originality, whatever it may have been, was shown by his power of interpreting the thoughts of his own age, then we can learn something from studying the social and intellectual position of his contemporaries. Though the individual remains inexplicable, the general characteristics of the school to which he belongs may be tolerably intelligible; and some explanation is in fact suggested by such epithets, for example, as romantic and classical. For, whatever precisely they mean,—and I confess to my mind the question of what they mean is often a very difficult one,—they imply some general tendency which cannot be attributed to individual influence. When we endeavour to approach this problem of the rise and fall of literary schools, we see that it is a case of a phenomenon which is very often noticed and which we are more ready to explain in proportion to the share of youthful audacity which we are fortunate enough to possess.

In every form of artistic production, in painting and architecture, for example, schools arise; each of which seems to embody some kind of principle, and develops and afterwards decays, according to some mysterious law. It may resemble the animal species which is, somehow or other, developed and then stamped out in the struggle of existence by the growth of a form more appropriate to the new order. The epic poem, shall we say? is like the 'monstrous efts,' as Tennyson unkindly calls them, which were no doubt very estimable creatures in their day, but have somehow been unable to adapt themselves to recent geological epochs. Why men could build cathedrals in the Middle Ages, and why their power was lost instead of steadily developing like the art of engineering, is a problem which has occupied many writers, and of which I shall not attempt to offer a solution. That is the difference between artistic and scientific progress. A truth once discovered remains true and may form the nucleus of an independently interesting body of truths. But a special form of art flourishes only during a limited period, and when it decays and is succeeded by others, we cannot say that there is necessarily progress, only that for some reason or other the environment has become uncongenial. It is, of course, tempting to infer from the decay of an art that there must be a corresponding decay in the vitality and morality of the race. Ruskin, for example, always assumed in his most brilliant and incisive, but not very conclusive, arguments that men ceased to paint good pictures simply because they ceased to be good men. He did not proceed to prove that the moral decline really took place, and still less to show why it took place. But, without attacking these large problems, I shall be content to say that I do not see that any such sweeping conclusions can be made as to the kind of changes in literary forms with which we shall be concerned. That there is a close relation between the literature and the general social condition of a nation is my own contention. But the relation is hardly of this simple kind. Nations, it seems to me, have got on remarkably well, and made not only material but political and moral progress in the periods when they have written few books, and those bad ones; and, conversely, have produced some admirable literature while they were developing some very ugly tendencies. To say the truth, literature seems to me to be a kind of by-product. It occupies far too small a part in the whole activity of a nation, even of its intellectual activity, to serve as a complete indication of the many forces which are at work, or as an adequate moral barometer of the general moral state. The attempt to establish such a condition too closely, seems to me to lead to a good many very edifying but not the less fallacious conclusions.

The succession of literary species implies that some are always passing into the stage of 'survivals': and the most obvious course is to endeavour to associate them with the general philosophical movement. That suggests one obvious explanation of many literary developments. The great thriving times of literature have occurred when new intellectual horizons seemed to be suddenly opening upon the human intelligence; as when Bacon was taking his Pisgah sight of the promised land of science, and Shakespeare and Spenser were making new conquests in the world of the poetic imagination. A great intellectual shock was stimulating the parallel, though independent, outbursts of activity. The remark may suggest one reason for the decline as well as for the rise of the new genus. If, on the one hand, the man of genius is especially sensitive to the new ideas which are stirring the world, it is also necessary that he should be in sympathy with his hearers—that he should talk the language which they understand, and adopt the traditions, conventions, and symbols with which they are already more or less familiar. A generally accepted tradition is as essential as the impulse which comes from the influx of new ideas. But the happy balance which enables the new wine to be put into the old bottles is precarious and transitory. The new ideas as they develop may become paralysing to the imagery which they began by utilising. The legends of chivalry which Spenser turned to account became ridiculous in the next generation, and the mythology of Milton's great poem was incredible or revolting to his successors. The machinery, in the old phrase, of a poet becomes obsolete, though when he used it, it had vitality enough to be a vehicle for his ideas. The imitative tendency described by Bagehot clearly tends to preserve the old, as much as to facilitate the adoption of a new form. In fact, to create a really original and new form seems to exceed the power of any individual, and the greatest men must desire to speak to their own contemporaries. It is only by degrees that the inadequacy of the traditional form makes itself felt, and its successor has to be worked out by a series of tentative experiments. When a new style has established itself its representatives hold that the orthodoxy of the previous period was a gross superstition: and those who were condemned as heretics were really prophets of the true faith, not yet revealed. However that may be, I am content at present to say that in fact the development of new literary types is discontinuous, and implies a compromise between the two conditions which in literature correspond to conservatism and radicalism. The conservative work is apt to become a mere survival: while the radical may include much that has the crudity of an imperfect application of new principles. Another point may be briefly indicated. The growth of new forms is obviously connected not only with the intellectual development but with the social and political state of the nation, and there comes into close connection with other departments of history. Authors, so far as I have noticed, generally write with a view to being read.

Moreover, the reading class is at most times a very small part of the population. A philosopher, I take it, might think himself unusually popular if his name were known to a hundredth part of the population. But even poets and novelists might sometimes be surprised if they could realise the small impression they make upon the mass of the population. There is, you know, a story of how Thackeray, when at the height of his reputation he stood for Oxford, found that his name was unknown even to highly respectable constituents. The author of *Vanity Fair* they observed, was named John Bunyan. At the present day the number of readers has, I presume, enormously increased ; but authors who can reach the lower strata of the great lower pyramid, which widens so rapidly at its base, are few indeed. The characteristics of a literature correspond to the national characteristics, as embodied in the characteristics of a very small minority of the nation. Two centuries ago the reading part of the nation was mainly confined to London and to certain classes of society. The most important changes which have taken place have been closely connected with the social changes which have entirely altered the limits of the reading class ;

and with the changes of belief which have been cause and effect of the most conspicuous political changes. That is too obvious to require any further exposition. Briefly, in talking of literary changes, considered as implied in the whole social development, I shall have, first, to take note of the main intellectual characteristics of the period; and secondly, what changes took place in the audience to which men of letters addressed themselves, and how the gradual extension of the reading class affected the development of the literature addressed to them.

I hope and believe that I have said nothing original. I have certainly only been attempting to express the views which are accepted, in their general outline at least, by historians, whether of the political or literary kind. They have often been applied very forcibly to the various literary developments, and, by way of preface to my own special topic, I will venture to recall one chapter of literary history which may serve to illustrate what I have already said, and which has a bearing upon what I shall have to say hereafter.

One of the topics upon which the newer methods of criticism first displayed their power was the school of the Elizabethan dramatists. Many of the earlier critics wrote like lovers or enthusiasts who exalted the merits of some of the old playwrights beyond our sober judgments, and were inclined to ignore the merits of other forms of the art. But we have come to recognise that the Elizabethans had their faults, and that the best apology for their weaknesses as well as the best explanation of their merits was to be found in a clearer appreciation of the whole conditions. It is impossible of course to overlook the connection between that great outburst of literary activity and the general movement of the time; of the period when many impulses were breaking up the old intellectual stagnation, and when the national spirit which took the great Queen for its representative was finding leaders in the Burleighs and Raleighs and Drakes. The connection is emphasised by the singular brevity of the literary efflorescence. Marlowe's *Tamburlaine* heralded its approach on the eve of the Spanish Armada: Shakespeare, to whom the lead speedily fell, had shown his highest power in *Henry IV.* and *Hamlet* before the accession of James I.: his great tragedies *Othello*, *Macbeth* and *Lear* were produced in the next two or three years; and by that time, Ben Jonson had done his best work.

When Shakespeare retired in 1611, Chapman and Webster, two of the most brilliant of his rivals, had also done their best; and Fletcher inherited the dramatic throne. On his death in 1625, Massinger and Ford and other minor luminaries were still at work; but the great period had passed. It had begun with the repulse of the Armada and culminated some fifteen years later. If in some minor respects there may afterwards have been an advance, the spontaneous vigour had declined and deliberate attempts to be striking had taken the place of the old audacity. There can be no more remarkable instance of a curious phenomenon, of a volcanic outburst of literary energy which begins and reaches its highest intensity while a man is passing from youth to middle age, and then begins to decay and exhaust itself within a generation.

A popular view used to throw the responsibility upon the wicked Puritans who used their power to close the theatres. We entered the 'prison-house' of Puritanism says Matthew Arnold, I think, and stayed there for a couple of centuries. If so, the gaolers must have had some difficulty, for the Puritan (in the narrower sense, of course) has always been in a small and unpopular minority. But it is also plain that the decay had begun when the Puritan was the victim instead of the inflictor of persecution. When we note the synchronism between the political and the literary movement our conception of the true nature of the change has to be modified. The accession of James marks the time at which the struggle between the court and the popular party was beginning to develop itself: when the monarchy and its adherents cease to represent the strongest current of national feeling, and the bulk of the most vigorous and progressive classes have become alienated and are developing the conditions and passions which produced the civil war. The genuine Puritans are still an exception; they only form the left wing, the most thorough-going opponents of the court-policy; and their triumph afterwards is only due to the causes which in a revolution give the advantage to the uncompromising partisans, though their special creed is always regarded with aversion by a majority. But for the time, they are the van of the party which, for whatever reason, is gathering strength and embodying the main political and ecclesiastical impulses of the time. The stage, again, had been from the first essentially aristocratic: it depended upon the court and the nobility and their adherents, and was hostile both to the Puritans and to the whole class in which the Puritan found a congenial element. So long, as in Elizabeth's time, as the class which supported the stage also represented the strongest aspirations of the period, and a marked national sentiment, the drama could embody a marked national sentiment. When the unity was broken up and the court is opposed to the strongest current of political sentiment, the players still adhere to their patron. The drama comes to represent a tone of thought, a social stratum, which, instead of leading, is getting more and more opposed to the great bulk of the most vigorous elements of the society. The stage is ceasing to be a truly national organ, and begins to suit itself to the tastes of the unprincipled and servile courtiers, who, if they are not more immoral than their predecessors, are without the old heroic touch which ennobled even the audacious and unscrupulous adventurers of the Armada period. That is to say, the change is beginning which became palpable in the Restoration time, when the stage became simply the melancholy dependent upon the court of Charles II., and faithfully reflected the peculiar morality of the small circle over which it presided. Without taking into account this process by which the organ of the nation gradually became transformed into the organ of the class which was entirely alienated from the general body of the nation, it is, I think, impossible to understand clearly the transformation of the drama. It illustrates the necessity of accounting for the literary movement, not only by intellectual and general causes, but by noting how special social developments radically alter the relation of any particular literary genus to the general national movement. I shall soon have to refer to the case again.

I have now only to say briefly what I propose to attempt in these lectures. The literary history, as I conceive it, is an account of one strand, so to speak, in a very complex tissue: it is connected with the intellectual and social development; it represents movements of thought which may sometimes check and be sometimes propitious to the existing forms of art; it is the utterance of a class which may represent, or fail to represent, the main national movement; it is affected more or less directly by all manner of religious, political, social, and economical changes; and it is dependent upon the occurrence of individual genius for which we cannot even profess to account. I propose to take the history of English literature in the eighteenth century. I do not aim at originality: I take for granted the ordinary critical judgments upon the great writers of whom so much has been said by judges certainly more competent than myself, and shall recall the same facts both of ordinary history and of the history of thought. What I hope is, that by bringing familiar facts together I may be able to bring out the nature of the connection between them; and, little as I can say that will be at all new, to illustrate one point of view, which, as I believe, it is desirable that literary histories should take into account more distinctly than they have generally done.

II

The first period of which I am to speak represents to the political historian the Avatar of Whiggism. The glorious revolution has decided the long struggle of the previous century; the main outlines of the British Constitution are irrevocably determined; the political system is in harmony with the great political forces, and the nation has settled, as Carlyle is fond of saying, with the centre of gravity lowest, and therefore in a position of stable equilibrium. For another century no organic change was attempted or desired. Parliament has become definitely the great driving-wheel of the political machinery; not, as a century before, an intrusive body acting spasmodically and hampering instead of regulating the executive power of the Crown. The last Stuart kings had still fancied that it might be reduced to impotence, and the illusion had been fostered by the loyalty which meant at least a fair unequivocal desire to hold to the old monarchical traditions. But, in fact, parliamentary control had been silently developing; the House of Commons had been getting the power of the purse more distinctly into its hands, and had taken very good care not to trust the Crown with the power of the sword. Charles II. had been forced to depend on the help of the great French monarchy to maintain his authority at home; and when his successor turned out to be an anachronism, and found that the loyalty of the nation would not bear the strain of a policy hostile to the strongest national impulses, he was thrown off as an intolerable incubus. The system which had been growing up beneath the surface was now definitely put into shape and its fundamental principles embodied in legislation. The one thing still needed was to work out the system of party government, which meant that parliament should become an organised body with a corporate body, which the ministers of the Crown had first to consult and then to obey. The essential parts of the system had, in fact, been established by the end of Queen Anne's reign; though the change which had taken place in the system was not fully recognised because marked by the retention of the old forms. This, broadly speaking, meant the supremacy of the class which really controlled Parliament: of the aristocratic class, led by the peers but including the body of squires and landed gentlemen, and including also a growing infusion of 'moneyed' men, who represented the rising commercial and manufacturing interests. The division between Whig and Tory corresponded mainly to the division between the men who inclined mainly to the Church and squirearchy and those who inclined towards the mercantile and the dissenting interests. If the Tory professed zeal for the monarchy, he did not mean a monarchy as opposed to Parliament and therefore to his own dearest privileges. Even the Jacobite movement was in great part personal, or meant dislike to Hanover with no preference for arbitrary power, while the actual monarchy was so far controlled by Parliament that the Whig had no desire to limit it further. It was a useful instrument, not an encumbrance.

We have to ask how these conditions affect the literary position. One point is clear. The relation between the political and the literary class was at this time closer than it had ever been. The alliance between them marks, in fact, a most conspicuous characteristic of the time. It was the one period, as authors repeat with a fond regret, in which literary merit was recognised by the distributors of state patronage. This gratifying phenomenon has, I think, been often a little misinterpreted, and I must consider briefly what it really meant. And first let us note how exclusively the literary society of the time was confined to London. The great town—it would be even now a great town—had half a million inhabitants. Macaulay, in his admirably graphic description of the England of the preceding period, points out what a chasm divided it from country districts; what miserable roads had to be traversed by the nobleman's chariot and four, or by the ponderous waggons or strings of pack-horses which supplied the wants of trade and of the humbler traveller; and how the squire only emerged at intervals to be jeered and jostled as an uncouth rustic in the streets of London. He was not a great buyer of books. There were, of course, libraries at Oxford and Cambridge, and here and there in the house of a rich prelate or of one of the great noblemen who were beginning to form some of the famous collections; but the squire was more than usually cultivated if Baker's *Chronicle* and Gwillim's *Heraldry* lay on the window-seat of his parlour, and one has often to wonder how the learned divines of the period managed to get the books from which they quote so freely in their discourses. Anyhow the author of the day must have felt that the circulation of his books must be mainly confined to London, and certainly in London alone could he meet with anything that could pass for literary society or an appreciative audience. We have superabundant descriptions of the audience and its meeting-places. One of the familiar features of the day, we know, was the number of coffee-houses. In 1657, we are told, the first coffee-house had been prosecuted as a nuisance. In 1708 there were three thousand coffee-houses; and each coffee-house had its habitual circle. There were coffee-houses frequented by merchants and stock-jobbers carrying on the game which suggested the new nickname bulls and bears: and coffee-houses where the talk was Whig and Tory, of the last election and change of ministry: and literary resorts such as the Grecian, where, as we are told, a fatal duel was provoked by a dispute over a Greek accent, in which, let us hope, it was the worst scholar who was killed; and Wills', where Pope as a boy went to look reverently at Dryden;

and Buttons', where, at a later period, Addison met his little senate. Addison, according to Pope, spent five or six hours a day lounging at Buttons'; while Pope found the practice and the consequent consumption of wine too much for his health. Thackeray notices how the club and coffee-house 'boozing shortened the lives and enlarged the waistcoats of the men of those days.' The coffee-house implied the club, while the club meant simply an association for periodical gatherings. It was only by degrees that the body made a permanent lodgment in the house and became first the tenants of the landlord and then themselves the proprietors. The most famous show the approximation between the statesmen and the men of letters. There was the great Kit-cat Club, of which Tonson the bookseller was secretary; to which belonged noble dukes and all the Whig aristocracy, besides Congreve, Vanbrugh, Addison, Garth, and Steele. It not only brought Whigs together but showed its taste by giving a prize for good comedies. Swift, when he came into favour, helped to form the Brothers' Club, which was especially intended to direct patronage towards promising writers of the Tory persuasion. The institution, in modern slang, differentiated as time went on. The more aristocratic clubs became exclusive societies, occupying their own houses, more devoted to gambling than to literature; while the older type, represented by Jonson's famous club, were composed of literary and professional classes.

The characteristic fraternisation of the politicians and the authors facilitated by this system leads to the critical point. When we speak of the nobility patronising literature, a reserve must be made. A list of some twenty or thirty names has been made out, including all the chief authors of the time, who received appointments of various kinds. But I can only find two, Congreve and Rowe, upon whom offices were bestowed simply as rewards for literary distinction; and both of them were sound Whigs, rewarded by their party, though not for party services. The typical patron of the day was Charles Montagu, Lord Halifax. As member of a noble family he came into Parliament, where he distinguished himself by his financial achievements in founding the Bank of England and reforming the currency, and became a peer and a member of the great Whig junto. At college he had been a chum of Prior, who joined him in a literary squib directed against Dryden, and, as he rose, he employed his friend in diplomacy. But the poetry by which Prior is known to us was of a later growth, and was clearly not the cause but the consequence of his preferment. At a later time, Halifax sent Addison abroad with the intention of employing him in a similar way; and it is plain that Addison was not—as the familiar but obviously distorted anecdote tells us—preferred on account of his brilliant Gazette in rhyme, but really in fulfilment of his patron's virtual pledge. Halifax has also the credit of bestowing office upon Newton and patronising Congreve. As poet and patron Halifax was carrying on a tradition. The aristocracy in Charles's days had been under the impression that poetry, or at least verse writing, was becoming an accomplishment for a nobleman. Pope's 'mob of gentlemen who wrote with ease,' Rochester and Buckingham, Dorset and Sedley, and the like, managed some very clever, if not very exalted, performances and were courted by the men of letters represented by Butler, Dryden, and Otway. As, indeed, the patrons were themselves hangers-on of a thoroughly corrupt court, seeking to rise by court intrigues, their patronage was apt to be degrading and involved the mean flattery of personal dependence. The change at the Revolution meant that the court no longer overshadowed society. The court, that is, was beginning to be superseded by the town. The new race of statesmen were coming to depend upon parliamentary influence instead of court favour. They were comparatively, therefore, shining by their own light. They were able to dispose of public appointments; places on the various commissions which had been founded as parliament took control of the financial system—such as commissions for the wine-duties, for licensing hackney coaches, excise duties, and so forth—besides some of the other places which had formerly been the perquisites of the courtier. They could reward personal dependants at the cost of the public; which was convenient for both parties. Promising university students, like Prior and Addison, might be brought out under the wing of the statesman, and no doubt literary merit, especially in conjunction with the right politics, might recommend them to such men as Halifax or Somers. The political power of the press was meanwhile rapidly developing. Harley, Lord Oxford, was one of the first to appreciate its importance. He employed Defoe and other humble writers who belonged to Grub Street—that is, to professional journalism in its infancy—as well as Swift, whose pamphlets struck the heaviest blow at the Whigs in the last years of that period. Swift's first writings, we may notice, were not a help but the main hindrance to his preferment. The patronage of literature was thus in great part political in its character. It represents the first scheme by which the new class of parliamentary statesmen recruited their party from the rising talent, or rewarded men for active or effective service. The speedy decay of the system followed for obvious reasons. As party government became organised, the patronage was used in a different spirit. Offices had to be given to gratify members of parliament and their constituents, not to scholars who could write odes on victories or epistles to secretaries of state. It was the machinery for controlling votes. Meanwhile we need only notice that the patronage of authors did not mean the patronage of learned divines or historians, but merely the patronage of men who could use their pens in political warfare, or at most of men who produced the kind of literary work appreciated in good society.

The 'town' was the environment of the wits who produced the literature generally called after Queen Anne. We may call it the literary organ of the society. It was the society of London, or of the region served by the new penny-post, which included such remote villages as Paddington and Brompton. The city was large enough, as Addison observes, to include numerous 'nations,' each of them meeting at the various coffee-houses. The clubs at which the politicians and authors met each other represented the critical tribunals, when no such things as literary journals existed. It was at these that judgment was passed upon the last new poem or pamphlet, and the writer sought for their good opinion as he now desires a favourable review. The tribunal included the rewarders as well as the judges of merit; and there was plenty of temptation to stimulate their generosity by flattery. Still the relation means a great improvement on the preceding state of things. The aristocrat was no doubt conscious of his inherent dignity, but he was ready on occasion to hail Swift as 'Jonathan' and, in the case of so highly cultivated a specimen as Addison, to accept an author's marriage to a countess. The patrons did not exact the personal subservience of the preceding period; and there was a real recognition by the more powerful class of literary merit of a certain order. Such a method, however, had obvious defects. Men of the world have their characteristic weaknesses; and one, to go no further, is significant. The Club in England corresponded more or less to the Salon which at different times had had so great an influence upon French literature. It differed in the marked absence of feminine elements. The clubs meant essentially a society of bachelors, and the conversation, one infers, was not especially suited for ladies. The Englishman, gentle or simple, enjoyed himself over his pipe and his bottle and dismissed his womenkind to their bed. The one author of the time who speaks of the influence of women with really chivalrous appreciation is the generous Steele, with his famous phrase about Lady Elizabeth Hastings and a liberal education. The Clubs did not foster the affectation of Molière's *Précieuses*; but the general tone had a coarseness and occasional brutality which shows too clearly that they did not enter into the full meaning of Steele's most admirable saying.

To appreciate the spirit of this society we must take into account the political situation and the intellectual implication. The parliamentary statesman, no longer dependent upon court favour, had a more independent spirit and personal self-respect. He was fully aware of the fact that he represented a distinct step in political progress. His class had won a great struggle against arbitrary power and bigotry. England had become the land of free speech, of religious toleration, impartial justice, and constitutional order. It had shown its power by taking its place among the leading European states. The great monarchy before which the English court had trembled, and from which even patriots had taken bribes in the Restoration period, was met face to face in a long and doubtful struggle and thoroughly humbled in a war, in which an English General, in command of an English contingent, had won victories unprecedented in our history since the Middle Ages. Patriotic pride received a stimulus such as that which followed the defeat of the Armada and preceded the outburst of the Elizabethan literature. Those successes, too, had been won in the name of 'liberty'—a vague if magical word which I shall not seek to define at present. England, so sound Whigs at least sincerely believed, had become great because it had adopted and carried out the true Whig principles. The most intelligent Frenchmen of the coming generation admitted the claim ; they looked upon England as the land both of liberty and philosophy, and tried to adopt for themselves the creed which had led to such triumphant results. One great name may tell us sufficiently what the principles were in the eyes of the cultivated classes, who regarded themselves and their own opinions with that complacency in which we are happily never deficient. Locke had laid down the fundamental outlines of the creed, philosophical, religious, and political, which was to dominate English thought for the next century. Locke was one of the most honourable, candid, and amiable of men, if metaphysicians have sometimes wondered at the success of his teaching. He had not the logical thoroughness and consistency which marks a Descartes or Spinoza, nor the singular subtlety which distinguishes Berkeley and Hume ; nor the eloquence and imaginative power which gave to Bacon an authority greater than was due to his scientific requirements. He was a thoroughly modest, prosaic, tentative, and sometimes clumsy writer, who raises great questions without solving them or fully seeing the consequences of his own position. Leaving any explanation of his power to metaphysicians, I need only note the most conspicuous condition. Locke ruled the thought of his own and the coming period because he interpreted so completely the fundamental beliefs which had been worked out at his time. He ruled, that is, by obeying. Locke represents the very essence of the common sense of the intelligent classes. I do not ask whether his simplicity covered really profound thought or embodied superficial crudities; but it was most admirably adapted to the society of which I have been speaking. The excellent Addison, for example, who was no metaphysician, can adopt Locke when he wishes to give a philosophical air to his amiable lectures upon arts and morals. Locke's philosophy, that is, blends spontaneously with the ordinary language of all educated men. To the historian of philosophy the period is marked by the final disappearance of scholasticism. The scholastic philosophy had of course been challenged generations before. Bacon, Descartes, and Hobbes, however, in the preceding century had still treated it as the great incubus upon intellectual progress, and it was not yet exorcised from the universities. It had, however, passed from the sphere of living thought. This implies a series of correlative changes in the social and intellectual which are equally conspicuous in the literary order, and which I must note without attempting to inquire which are the ultimate or most fundamental causes of reciprocally related developments. The changed position of the Anglican church is sufficiently significant. In the time of Laud, the bishops in alliance with the Crown endeavoured to enforce the jurisdiction of the ecclesiastical courts upon the nation at large, and to suppress all nonconformity by law. Every subject of the king is also amenable to church discipline. By the Revolution any attempt to enforce such discipline had become hopeless. The existence of nonconformist churches has to be recognised as a fact, though perhaps an unpleasant fact. The Dissenters can be worried by disqualifications of various kinds ; but the claim to toleration, of Protestant sects at least, is admitted ; and the persecution is political rather than ecclesiastical. They are not regarded as heretics, but as representing an interest which is opposed to the dominant class of the landed gentry. The Church as such has lost the power of discipline and is gradually falling under the power of the dominant aristocratic class. When Convocation tries to make itself troublesome, in a few years, it will be silenced and drop into impotence. Church-feeling indeed, is still strong, but the clergy have become thoroughly subservient, and during the century will be mere appendages to the nobility and squirearchy. The intellectual change is parallel. The great divines of the seventeenth century speak as members of a learned corporation condescending to instruct the laity. The hearers are supposed to listen to the voice (as Donne puts it) as from 'angels in the clouds.' They are experts, steeped in a special science, above the comprehension of the vulgar. They have been trained in the schools of theology and have been thoroughly drilled in the art of 'syllogising.' They are walking libraries with the ancient fathers at their finger-ends; they have studied Aquinas and Duns Scotus, and have shown their technical knowledge in controversies with the great Jesuits, Suarez and Bellarmine. They speak frankly, if not ostentatiously, as men of learning, and their sermons are overweighted with quotations, showing familiarity with the classics, and with the whole range of theological literature. Obviously the hearers are to be passive recipients not judges of the doctrine. But by the end of the century Tillotson has become the typical divine, whose authority was to be as marked in theology as that of Locke in philosophy. Tillotson has entirely abandoned any ostentatious show of learning. He addresses his hearers in language on a level with their capabilities, and assumes that they are not 'passive buckets to be pumped into' but reasonable men who have a right to be critics as well as disciples. It is taken for granted that the appeal must be to reason, and to the reason which has not gone through any special professional training. The audience, that is, to which the divine must address himself is one composed of the average laity who are quite competent to judge for themselves. That is the change that is meant when we are told that this was the period of the development of English prose. Dryden, one of its great masters, professed to have learned his style from Tillotson. The writer, that is, has to suit himself to the new audience which has grown up. He has to throw aside all the panoply of scholastic logic, the vast apparatus of professional learning, and the complex Latinised constructions, which, however admirable some of the effects produced, shows that the writer is thinking of well-read scholars, not of the ordinary man of the world. He has learned from Bacon and Descartes, perhaps, that his supposed science was useless lumber; and he has to speak to men who not only want plain language but are quite convinced that the pretensions of the old authority have been thoroughly exploded.

Politically, the change means toleration, for it is assumed that the vulgar can judge for themselves; intellectually, it means rationalism, that is, an appeal to the reason common to all men; and, in literature it means the hatred of pedantry and the acceptance of such literary forms as are thoroughly congenial and intelligible to the common sense of the new audience. The hatred of the pedantic is the characteristic sentiment of the time. When Berkeley looked forward to a new world in America, he described it as the Utopia

> 'Where men shall not impose for truth and sense
> The pedantry of Courts and Schools.'

When he announced a metaphysical discovery he showed his understanding of the principle by making his exposition—strange as the proceeding appears to us—as short and as clear as the most admirable literary skill could contrive. That eccentric ambition dominates the writings of the times. In a purely literary direction it is illustrated by the famous but curiously rambling and equivocal controversy about the Ancients and Moderns begun in France by Perrault and Boileau. In England the most familiar outcome was Swift's *Battle of the Books*, in which he struck out the famous phrase about sweetness and light, 'the two noblest of things'; which he illustrated by ridiculing Bentley's criticism and Dryden's poetry. I may take for granted the motives which induced that generation to accept as their models the great classical masterpieces, the study of which had played so important a part in the revival of letters and the new philosophy. I may perhaps note, in passing, that we do not always remember what classical literature meant to that generation. In the first place, the education of a gentleman meant nothing then except a certain drill in Greek and Latin—whereas now it includes a little dabbling in other branches of knowledge. In the next place, if a man had an appetite for literature, what else was he to read? Imagine every novel, poem, and essay written during the last two centuries to be obliterated—and further, the literature of the early seventeenth century and all that went before to be regarded as pedantic and obsolete, the field of study would be so limited that a man would be forced in spite of himself to read his *Homer* and *Virgil.* The vice of pedantry was not very accurately defined—sometimes it is the ancient, sometimes the modern, who appears to be pedantic. Still, as in the *Battle of the Books* controversy, the general opinion seems to be that the critic should have before him the great classical models, and regard the English literature of the seventeenth century as a collection of all possible errors of taste. When, at the end of this period, Swift with Pope formed the project of the Scriblerus Club, its aim was to be a joint-stock satire against all 'false tastes' in learning, art, and science. That was the characteristic conception of the most brilliant men of letters of the time.

Here, then, we have the general indication of the composition of the literary organ. It is made up of men of the world—'Wits' is their favourite self-designation, scholars and gentlemen, with rather more of the gentlemen than the scholars—living in the capital, which forms a kind of island of illumination amid the surrounding darkness of the agricultural country—including men of rank and others of sufficient social standing to receive them on friendly terms—meeting at coffee-houses and in a kind of tacit confederation of clubs to compare notes and form the whole public opinion of the day. They are conscious that in them is concentrated the enlightenment of the period. The class to which they belong is socially and politically dominant—the advance guard of national progress. It has finally cast off the incubus of a retrograde political system; it has placed the nation in a position of unprecedented importance in Europe; and it is setting an example of ordered liberty to the whole civilised world. It has forced the Church and the priesthood to abandon the old claim to spiritual supremacy. It has, in the intellectual sphere, crushed the old authority which embodied superstition, antiquated prejudice, and a sham system of professional knowledge, which was upheld by a close corporation. It believes in reason—meaning the principles which are evident to the ordinary common sense of men at its own level. It believes in what it calls the Religion of Nature—the plain demonstrable truths obvious to every intelligent person. With Locke for its spokesman, and Newton as a living proof of its scientific capacity, it holds that England is the favoured nation marked out as the land of liberty, philosophy, common sense, toleration, and intellectual excellence. And with certain reserves, it will be taken at its own valuation by foreigners who are still in darkness and deplorably given to slavery, to say nothing of wooden shoes and the consumption of frogs. Let us now consider the literary result.

I may begin by recalling a famous controversy which seems to illustrate very significantly some of the characteristic tendencies of the day. The stage, when really flourishing, might be expected to show most conspicuously the relations between authors and the society. The dramatist may be writing for all time ; but if he is to fill a theatre, he must clearly adapt himself to the tastes of the living and the present. During the first half of the period of which I am now speaking, Dryden was still the dictator of the literary world ; and Dryden had adopted Congreve as his heir, and abandoned to him the province of the drama—Congreve, though he ceased to write, was recognised during his life as the great man of letters to whom Addison, Swift, and Pope agreed in paying respect, and indisputably the leading writer of English Comedy. When the comic drama was unsparingly denounced by Collier, Congreve defended himself and his friends. In the judgment of contemporaries the pedantic parson won a complete triumph over the most brilliant of wits. Although Congreve's early abandonment of his career was not caused by Collier's attack alone, it was probably due in part to the general sentiment to which Collier gave utterance. I will ask what is implied as a matter of fact in regard to the social and literary characteristics of the time. The Shakespearian drama had behind it a general national impulse. With Fletcher, it began to represent a court already out of harmony with the strongest currents of national feeling. Dryden, in a familiar passage, gives the reason of the change from his own point of view. Two plays of Beaumont and Fletcher, he says in an often quoted passage, were acted (about 1668) for one of Shakespeare or Jonson. His explanation is remarkable. It was because the later dramatists 'understood the conversation of gentlemen much better,' whose wild 'debaucheries and quickness of wit no poet can ever paint as they have done.' In a later essay he explains that the greater refinement was due to the influence of the court. Charles II., familiar with the most brilliant courts of Europe, had roused us from barbarism and rebellion, and taught us to 'mix our solidity' with 'the air and gaiety of our neighbours'! I need not cavil at the phrases 'refinement' and 'gentleman.' If those words can be fairly applied to the courtiers whose 'wild debaucheries' disgusted Evelyn and startled even the respectable Pepys, they may no doubt be applied to the stage and the dramatic persons. The rake, or 'wild gallant,' had made his first appearance in Fletcher, and had shown himself more nakedly after the Restoration. This is the so-called reaction so often set down to the account of the unlucky Puritans. The degradation, says Macaulay, was the 'effect of the prevalence of Puritanism under the Commonwealth.' The attempt to make a 'nation of saints' inevitably produced a nation of scoffers. In what sense, in the first place, was there a 'reaction' at all? The Puritans had suppressed the stage when it was already far gone in decay because it no longer satisfied the great bulk of the nation. The reaction does not imply that the drama regained its old position. When the rule of the saints or pharisees was broken down, the stage did not become again a national organ. A very small minority of the people can ever have seen a performance. There were, we must remember, only two theatres under Charles II., and there was a difficulty in supporting even two. Both depended almost exclusively on the patronage of the court and the courtiers. From the theatre, therefore, we can only argue directly to the small circle of the rowdy debauchees who gathered round the new king. It certainly may be true, but it was not proved from their behaviour, that the national morality deteriorated, and in fact I think nothing is more difficult than to form any trustworthy estimate of the state of morality in a whole nation, confidently as such estimates are often put forward. What may be fairly inferred, is that a certain class, who had got from under the rule of the Puritan, was now free from legal restraint and took advantage of the odium excited by pharisaical strictness, to indulge in the greater license which suited the taste of their patrons. The result is sufficiently shown when we see so great a man as Dryden pander to the lowest tastes, and guilty of obscenities of which he was himself ashamed, which would be now inexcusable in the lowest public haunts.

The comedy, as it appears to us, must have been written by blackguards for blackguards. When Congreve became Dryden's heir he inherited the established tradition. Under the new order the 'town' had become supreme; and Congreve wrote to meet the taste of the class which was gaining in self-respect and independence. He tells us in the dedication of his best play, *The Way of the World*, that his taste had been refined in the company of the Earl of Montagu. The claim is no doubt justifiable. So Horace Walpole remarks that Vanbrugh wrote so well because he was familiar with the conversation of the best circles. The social influences were favourable to the undeniable literary merits, to the force and point in which Congreve's dialogue is still superior to that of any English rival, the vigour of Vanbrugh and the vivacity of their chief ally, Farquhar. Moreover, although their moral code is anything but strict, these writers did not descend to some of the depths often sounded by Dryden and Wycherly. The new spirit might seem to be passing on with more literary vitality into the old forms. And yet the consequence, or certainly the sequel to Collier's attack, was the decay of the stage in every sense, from which there was no recovery till the time of Goldsmith and Sheridan.

This is the phenomenon which we have to consider ;—let us listen for a moment to the 'distinguished critics' who have denounced or defended the comedy of the time. Macaulay gives as a test of the morality of the Restoration stage that on it, for the first time, marriage becomes the topic of ridicule. We are supposed to sympathise with the adulterer, not with the deceived husband—a fault, he says, which stains no play written before the Civil War. Addison had already suggested this test in the *Spectator*, and proceeds to lament that 'the multitudes are shut out from this noble "diversion" by the immorality of the lessons inculcated.' Lamb, indulging in ingenious paradox, admires Congreve for 'excluding from his scenes (with one exception) any pretensions to goodness or good feeling whatever.' Congreve, he says, spreads a 'privation of moral light' over his characters, and therefore we can admire them without compunction. We are in an artificial world where we can drop our moral prejudices for the time being. Hazlitt more daringly takes a different position and asserts that one of Wycherly's coarsest plays is 'worth ten sermons'—which perhaps does not imply with him any high estimate of moral efficacy. There is, however, this much of truth, I take it, in Hazlitt's contention. Lamb's theory of the non-morality of the dramatic world will not stand examination. The comedy was in one sense thoroughly 'realistic'; and I am inclined to say, that in that lay its chief merit. There is some value in any truthful representation, even of vice and brutality. There would certainly be no difficulty in finding flesh and blood originals for the rakes and the fine ladies in the memoirs of Grammont or the diaries of Pepys. The moral atmosphere is precisely that of the dissolute court of Charles II., and the 'privation of moral light' required is a delicate way of expressing its characteristic feeling. In the worst performances we have not got to any unreal region, but are breathing for the time the atmosphere of the lowest resorts, where reference to pure or generous sentiment would undoubtedly have been received with a guffaw, and coarse cynicism be regarded as the only form of comic insight. At any rate the audiences for which Congreve wrote had just so much of the old leaven that we can quite understand why they were regarded as wicked by a majority of the middle classes. The doctrine that all playgoing was wicked was naturally confirmed, and the dramatists retorted by ridiculing all that their enemies thought respectable. Congreve was, I fancy, a man of better morality than his characters, only forced to pander to the tastes of the rake who had composed the dominant element of his audience. He writes not for mere blackguards, but for the fine gentleman, who affects premature knowledge of the world, professes to be more cynical than he really is, and shows his acuteness by deriding hypocrisy and pharisaic humbug in every claim to virtue. He dwells upon the seamy side of life, and if critics, attracted by his undeniable brilliance, have found his heroines charming, to me it seems that they are the kind of young women whom, if I adopted his moral code, I should think most desirable wives—for my friends.

Though realistic in one sense, we may grant to Lamb that such comedy becomes 'artificial,' and so far Lamb is right, because it supposes a state of things such as happily was abnormal except in a small circle. The plots have to be made up of impossible intrigues, and imply a distorted theory of life. Marriage after all is not really ridiculous, and to see it continuously from this point of view is to have a false picture of realities. Life is not made up of dodges worthy of cardsharpers—and the whole mechanism becomes silly and disgusting. If comedy is to represent a full and fair portrait of life, the dramatist ought surely, in spite of Lamb, to find some space for generous and refined feeling. There, indeed, is a difficulty. The easiest way to be witty is to be cynical. It is difficult, though desirable, to combine good feeling with the comic spirit. The humourist has to expose the contrasts of life, to unmask hypocrisy, and to show selfishness lurking under multitudinous disguises. That, on Hazlitt's showing, was the preaching of Wycherly. I can't think that it was the impression made upon Wycherly's readers. Such comedy may be taken as satire; which was the excuse that Fielding afterwards made for his own performances. But I cannot believe that the actual audiences went to see vice exposed, or used Lamb's ingenious device of disbelieving in the reality. They simply liked brutal and immoral sentiment, spiced, if possible, with art. We may inquire whether there may not be a comedy which is enjoyable by the refined and virtuous, and in which the intrusion of good feeling does not jar upon us as a discord. An answer may be suggested by pointing to Molière, and has been admirably set forth in Mr. George Meredith's essay on the 'Comic Spirit.' There are, after all, ridiculous things in the world, even from the refined and virtuous point of view. The saint, it is true, is apt to lose his temper and become too serious for such a treatment of life-problems. Still the sane intellect which sees things as they are can find a sphere within which it is fair and possible to apply ridicule to affectation and even to vice, and without simply taking the seat of the scorner or substituting a coarse laugh for a delicate smile. A hearty laugh, let us hope, is possible even for a fairly good man. Mr. Meredith's essay indicates the conditions under which the artist may appeal to such a cultivated and refined humour. The higher comedy, he says, can only be the fruit of a polished society which can supply both the model and the audience. Where the art of social intercourse has been carried to a high pitch, where men have learned to be at once courteous and incisive, to admire urbanity, and therefore really good feeling, and to take a true estimate of the real values of life, a high comedy which can produce irony without coarseness, expose shams without advocating brutality, becomes for the first time possible. It must be admitted that the condition is also very rarely fulfilled.

This, I take it, is the real difficulty. The desirable thing, one may say, would have been to introduce a more refined and human art and to get rid of the coarser elements. The excellent Steele tried the experiment. But he had still to work upon the old lines, which would not lend themselves to the new purpose. His passages of moral exhortation would not supply the salt of the old cynical brutalities; they had a painful tendency to become insipid and sentimental, if not maudlin; and only illustrated the difficulty of using a literary tradition which developed spontaneously for one purpose to adapt itself to a wholly different aim. He produced at best not a new genus but an awkward hybrid. But behind this was the greater difficulty that a superior literature would have required a social elaboration, the growth of a class which could appreciate and present appropriate types. Now even the good society for which Congreve wrote had its merits, but certainly its refinement left much to be desired. One condition, as Mr. Meredith again remarks, of the finer comedy is such an equality of the sexes as may admit the refining influence of women. The women of the Restoration time hardly exerted a refining influence. They adopted the ingenious compromise of going to the play, but going in masks. That is, they tacitly implied that the brutality was necessary, and they submitted to what they could not openly approve. Throughout the eighteenth century a contempt for women was still too characteristic of the aristocratic character. Nor was there any marked improvement in the tastes of the playgoing classes. The plays denounced by Collier continued to hold the stage, though more or less expurgated, throughout the century. Comedy did not become decent. In 1729 Arthur Bedford carried on Collier's assault in a 'Remonstrance against the horrid blasphemies and improprieties which are still used in the English playhouses,' and collected seven thousand immoral sentiments from the plays (chiefly) of the last four years. I have not verified his statements. The inference, however, seems to be clear. Collier's attack could not reform the stage. The evolution took the form of degeneration. He could, indeed, give utterance to the disapproval of the stage in general, which we call Puritanical, though it was by no means confined to Puritans or even to Protestants. Bossuet could denounce the stage as well as Collier. Collier was himself a Tory and a High Churchman, as was William Law, of the *Serious Call*, who also denounced the stage. The sentiment was, in fact, that of the respectable middle classes in general. The effect was to strengthen the prejudice which held that playgoing was immoral in itself, and that an actor deserved to be treated as a 'vagrant'—the class to which he legally belonged. During the next half-century, at least, that was the prevailing opinion among the solid middle-class section of society.

The denunciations of Collier and his allies certainly effected a reform, but at a heavy price. They did not elevate the stage or create a better type, but encouraged old prejudices against the theatre generally; the theatre was left more and more to a section of the 'town,' and to the section which was not too particular about decency. When Congreve retired, and Vanbrugh took to architecture, and Farquhar died, no adequate successors appeared. The production of comedies was left to inferior writers, to Mrs. Centlivre, and Colley Cibber, and Fielding in his unripe days, and they were forced by the disfavour into which their art had fallen to become less forcible rather than to become more refined. When a preacher denounces the wicked, his sermons seem to be thrown away because the wicked don't come to church. Collier could not convert his antagonists; he could only make them more timid and careful to avoid giving palpable offence. But he could express the growing sentiment which made the drama an object of general suspicion and dislike, and induced the ablest writers to turn to other methods for winning the favour of a larger public.

The natural result, in fact, was the development of a new kind of literature, which was the most characteristic innovation of the period. The literary class of which I have hitherto spoken reflected the opinions of the upper social stratum. Beneath it was the class generally known as Grub Street. Grub Street had arisen at the time of the great civil struggle. War naturally generates journalism; it had struggled on through the Restoration and taken a fresh start at the Revolution and the final disappearance of the licensing system. The daily newspaper—meaning a small sheet written by a single author (editors as yet were not)—appeared at the opening of the eighteenth century. Now for Grub Street the wit of the higher class had nothing but dislike. The 'hackney author,' as Dunton called him, in his curious *Life and Errors*, was a mere huckster, who could scarcely be said as yet to belong to a profession. A Tutchin or Defoe might be pilloried, or flogged, or lose his ears, without causing a touch of compassion from men like Swift, who would have disdained to call themselves brother authors. Yet politicians were finding him useful. He was the victim of one party, and might be bribed or employed as a spy by the other. The history of Defoe and his painful struggles between his conscience and his need of living, sufficiently indicates the result; Charles Leslie, the gallant nonjuror, for example, or Abel Boyer, the industrious annalist, or the laborious but cantankerous Oldmixon, were keeping their heads above water by journalism, almost exclusively, of course, political. Defoe showed a genius for the art, and his mastery of vigorous vernacular was hardly rivalled until the time of Paine and Cobbett. At any rate, it was plain that a market was now arising for periodical literature which might give a scanty support to a class below the seat of patrons. It was at this point that the versatile, speculative, and impecunious Steele hit upon his famous discovery. The aim of the *Tatler*, started in April 1709, was marked out with great accuracy from the first. Its purpose is to contain discourses upon all manner of topics—*quicquid agunt homines*, as his first motto put it—which had been inadequately treated in the daily papers. It is supposed to be written in the various coffee-houses, and it is suited to all classes, even including women, whose taste, he observes, is to be caught by the title. The *Tatler*, as we know, led to the *Spectator*, and Addison's co-operation, cordially acknowledged by his friend, was a main cause of its unprecedented success. The *Spectator* became the model for at least three generations of writers. The number of imitations is countless: Fielding, Johnson, Goldsmith, and many men of less fame tried to repeat the success; persons of quality, such as Chesterfield and Horace Walpole, condescended to write papers for the *World*—the 'Bow of Ulysses,' as it was called, in which they could test their strength. Even in the nineteenth century Hazlitt and Leigh Hunt carried on the form ; as indeed, in a modified shape, many later essayists have aimed at a substantially similar achievement. To have contributed three or four articles was, as in the case of the excellent Henry Grove (a name, of course, familiar to all of you), to have graduated with honours in literature. Johnson exhorted the literary aspirant to give his days and nights to the study of Addison ; and the *Spectator* was the most indispensable set of volumes upon the shelves of every library where the young ladies described by Miss Burney and Miss Austen were permitted to indulge a growing taste for literature. I fear that young people of the present day discover, if they try the experiment, that their curiosity is easily satisfied. This singular success, however, shows that the new form satisfied a real need. Addison's genius must, of course, count for much in the immediate result ; but it was plainly a case where genius takes up the function for which it is best suited, and in which it is most fully recognised. When we read him now we are struck by one fact. He claims in the name of the *Spectator* to be a censor of manners and morals ; and though he veils his pretensions under delicate irony, the claim is perfectly serious at bottom. He is really seeking to improve and educate his readers. He aims his gentle ridicule at social affectations and frivolities; and sometimes, though avoiding ponderous satire, at the grosser forms of vice. He is not afraid of laying down an æsthetic theory. In a once famous series of papers on the Imagination, he speaks with all the authority of a recognised critic in discussing the merits of Chevy Chase or of *Paradise Lost*; and in a series of Saturday papers he preaches lay-sermons—which were probably preferred by many readers to the official discourses of the following day. They contain those striking poems (too few) which led Thackeray to say that he could hardly fancy a 'human intellect thrilling with a purer love and admiration than Joseph Addison's.' Now, spite of the real charm which every lover of delicate humour and exquisite urbanity must find in Addison, I fancy that the *Spectator* has come to mean for us chiefly Sir Roger de Coverley. It is curious, and perhaps painful, to note how very small a proportion of the whole is devoted to that most admirable achievement; and to reflect how little life there is in much that in kindness of feeling and grace of style is equally charming. One cause is obvious. When Addison talks of psychology or æsthetics or ethics (not to speak of his criticism of epic poetry or the drama), he must of course be obsolete in substance; but, moreover, he is obviously superficial. A man who would speak upon such topics now must be a grave philosopher, who has digested libraries of philosophy. Addison, of course, is the most modest of men; he has not the slightest suspicion that he is going beyond his tether; and that is just what makes his unconscious audacity remarkable. He fully shares the characteristic belief of the day, that the abstract problems are soluble by common sense, when polished by academic culture and aided by a fine taste. It is a case of *sancta simplicitas*; of the charming, because perfectly unconscious, self-sufficiency with which the Wit, rejecting pedantry as the source of all evil, thinks himself obviously entitled to lay down the law as theologian, politician, and philosopher. His audience are evidently ready to accept him as an authority, and are flattered by being treated as capable of reason, not offended by any assumption of their intellectual inferiority.

With whatever shortcomings, Addison, and in their degree Steele and his other followers, represent the stage at which the literary organ begins to be influenced by the demands of a new class of readers. Addison feels the dignity of his vocation and has a certain air of gentle condescension, especially when addressing ladies who cannot even translate his mottoes. He is a genuine prophet of what we now describe as Culture, and his exquisite urbanity and delicacy qualify him to be a worthy expositor of the doctrines, though his outlook is necessarily limited. He is therefore implicitly trying to solve the problem which could not be adequately dealt with on the stage; to set forth a view of the world and human nature which shall be thoroughly refined and noble, and yet imply a full appreciation of the humorous aspects of life. The inimitable Sir Roger embodies the true comic spirit; though Addison's own attempt at comedy was not successful.

One obvious characteristic of this generation is the didacticism which is apt to worry us. Poets, as well as philosophers and preachers, are terribly argumentative. Fielding's remark (through Parson Adams), that some things in Steele's comedies are almost as good as a sermon, applies to a much wider range of literature. One is tempted by way of explanation to ascribe this to a primitive and ultimate instinct of the race. Englishmen—including of course Scotsmen—have a passion for sermons, even when they are half ashamed of it; and the British Essay, which flourished so long, was in fact a lay sermon. We must briefly notice that the particular form of this didactic tendency is a natural expression of the contemporary rationalism. The metaphysician of the time identifies emotions and passions with intellectual affirmations, and all action is a product of logic. In any case we have to do with a period in which the old concrete imagery has lost its hold upon the more intelligent classes, and instead of an imaginative symbolism we have a system of abstract reasoning. Diagrams take the place of concrete pictures: and instead of a Milton justifying the ways of Providence by the revealed history, we have a Blackmore arguing with Lucretius, and are soon to have a Pope expounding a metaphysical system in the *Essay on Man*. Sir Roger represents a happy exception to this method and points to the new development. Addison is anticipating the method of later novelists, who incarnate their ideals in flesh and blood. This, and the minor character sketches which are introduced incidentally, imply a feeling after a less didactic method. As yet the sermon is in the foreground, and the characters are dismissed as soon as they have illustrated the preacher's doctrine. Such a method was congenial to the Wit. He was, or aspired to be, a keen man of the world; deeply interested in the characteristics of the new social order; in the eccentricities displayed at clubs, or on the Stock Exchange, or in the political struggles; he is putting in shape the practical philosophy implied in the conversations at clubs and coffee-houses; he delights in discussing such psychological problems as were suggested by the worldly wisdom of Rochefoucauld, and he appreciates clever character sketches such as those of La Bruyére. Both writers were favourites in England. But he has become heartily tired of the old romance, and has not yet discovered how to combine the interest of direct observation of man with a thoroughly concrete form of presentation.

The periodical essay represents the most successful innovation of the day; and, as I have suggested, because it represents the mode by which the most cultivated writer could be brought into effective relation with the genuine interests of the largest audience. Other writers used it less skilfully, or had other ways of delivering their message to mankind. Swift, for example, had already shown his peculiar vein. He gives a different, though equally characteristic, side of the intellectual attitude of the Wit. In the *Battle of the Books* he had assumed the pedantry of the scholar; in the *Tale of a Tub* with amazing audacity he fell foul of the pedantry of divines. His blows, as it seemed to the Archbishops, struck theology in general; he put that right by pouring out scorn upon Deists and all who were silly enough to believe that the vulgar could reason; and then in his first political writings began to expose the corrupt and selfish nature of politicians—though at present only of Whig politicians. Swift is one of the most impressive of all literary figures, and I will not even touch upon his personal peculiarities. I will only remark that in one respect he agrees with his friend Addison. He emphasises, of course, the aspect over which Addison passes lightly; he scorns fools too heartily to treat them tenderly and do justice to the pathetic side of even human folly. But he too believes in culture—though he may despair of its dissemination. He did his best, during his brief period of power, to direct patronage towards men of letters, even to Whigs; and tried, happily without success, to found an English Academy. His zeal was genuine, though it expressed itself by scorn for dunces and hostility to Grub Street. He illustrates one little peculiarity of the Wit. In the society of the clubs there was a natural tendency to form minor cliques of the truly initiated, who looked with sovereign contempt upon the hackney author. One little indication is the love of mystifications, or what were entitled 'bites.' All the Wits, as we know, combined to tease the unlucky fortune-teller, Partridge, and to maintain that their prediction of his death had been verified, though he absurdly pretended to be still alive. So Swift tells us in the journal to Stella how he had circulated a lie about a man who had been hanged coming to life again, and how footmen are sent out to inquire into its success. He made a hit by writing a sham account of Prior's mission to Paris supposed to come from a French valet. The inner circle chuckled over such performances, which would be impossible when their monopoly of information had been broken up. A similar satisfaction was given by the various burlesques and more or less ingenious fables which were to be fully appreciated by the inner circle ; such as the tasteless narrative of Dennis's frenzy by which Pope professed to be punishing his victim for an attack upon Addison : or to such squibs as Arbuthnot's *John Bull*—a parable which gives the Tory view in a form fitted for the intelligent. The Wits, that is, form an inner circle, who like to speak with an affectation of obscurity even if the meaning be tolerably transparent, and show that they are behind the scenes by occasionally circulating bits of sham news. They like to form a kind of select upper stratum, which most fully believes in its own intellectual eminence, and shows a contempt for its inferiors by burlesque and rough sarcasm.

It is not difficult (especially when we know the result) to guess at the canons of taste which will pass muster in such regions. Enthusiastical politicians of recent days have been much given to denouncing modern clubs, where everybody is a cynic and unable to appreciate the great ideas which stir the masses. It may be so ; my own acquaintance with club life, though not very extensive, does not convince me that every member of a London club is a Mephistopheles ; but I will admit that a certain excess of hard worldly wisdom may be generated in such resorts ;

and we find many conspicuous traces of that tendency in the clubs of Queen Anne's reign. Few of them have Addison's gentleness or his perception of the finer side of human nature. It was by a rare combination of qualities that he was enabled to write like an accomplished man of the world, and yet to introduce the emotional element without any jarring discord. The literary reformers of a later day denounce the men of this period as 'artificial'! a phrase the antithesis of which is 'natural.' Without asking at present what is meant by the implied distinction—an inquiry which is beset by whole systems of equivocations—I may just observe that in this generation the appeal to Nature was as common and emphatic as in any later time. The leaders of thought believe in reason, and reason sets forth the Religion of Nature and assumes that the Law of Nature is the basis of political theory. The corresponding literary theory is that Art must be subordinate to Nature. The critics' rules, as Pope says in the poem which most fully expresses the general doctrine,

> 'Are Nature still, but Nature methodised ;
> Nature, like Liberty, is but restrained
> By the same laws which first herself ordained.'

The Nature thus 'methodised' was the nature of the Wit himself; the set of instincts and prejudices which to him seemed to be so normal that they must be natural. Their standards of taste, if artificial to us, were spontaneous, not fictitious; the Wits were not wearing a mask, but were exhibiting their genuine selves with perfect simplicity. Now one characteristic of the Wit is always a fear of ridicule. Above all things he dreads making a fool of himself. The old lyric, for example, which came so spontaneously to the Elizabethan poet or dramatist, and of which echoes are still to be found in the Restoration, has decayed, or rather, has been transformed. When you have written a genuine bit of love-poetry, the last place, I take it, in which you think of seeking the applause of a congenial audience, would be the smoking-room of your club: but that is the nearest approach to the critical tribunal of Queen Anne's day. It is necessary to smuggle in poetry and passion in disguise, and conciliate possible laughter by stating plainly that you anticipate the ridicule yourself. In other words you write society verses like Prior, temper sentiment by wit, and if you do not express vehement passion, turn out elegant verses, salted by an irony which is a tacit apology perhaps for some genuine feeling. The old pastoral had become hopelessly absurd because Thyrsis and Lycidas have become extravagant and 'unnatural.' The form might be adopted for practice in versification; but when Ambrose Phillips took it a little too seriously, Pope, whose own performances were not much better, came down on him for his want of sincerity, and Gay showed what could be still made of the form by introducing real rustics and turning it into a burlesque. Then, as Johnson puts it, the 'effect of reality and truth became conspicuous, even when the intention was to show them grovelling and degraded.' *The Rape of the Lock* is the masterpiece, as often noticed, of an unconscious allegory. The sylph, who was introduced with such curious felicity, is to be punished if he fails to do his duty, by imprisonment in a lady's toilet apparatus.

> 'Gums and pomatums shall his flight restrain,
> While clogged he beats his silver wings in vain.'

Delicate fancy and real poetical fancy may be turned to account; but under the mask of the mock-heroic. We can be poetical still, it seems to say, only we must never forget that to be poetical in deadly earnest is to run the risk of being absurd. Even a Wit is pacified when he is thus dexterously coaxed into poetry disguised as mere playful exaggeration, and feels quite safe in following the fortune of a game of cards in place of a sanguinary Homeric battle. Ariel is still alive, but he adopts the costume of the period to apologise for his eccentricities. Poetry thus understood may either give a charm to the trivial or fall into mere burlesque; and though Pope's achievement is an undeniable triumph, there are blots in an otherwise wonderful performance which show an uncomfortable concession to the coarser tastes of his audience.

I will not dwell further upon a tolerably obvious theme. I must pass to the more serious literature. The Wit had not the smallest notion that his attitude disqualified him for succession in the loftiest poetical endeavour. He thinks that his critical keenness will enable him to surpass the old models. He wishes, in the familiar phrase, to be 'correct'; to avoid the gross faults of taste which disfigured the old Gothic barbarism of his forefathers. That for him is the very meaning of reason and nature. He will write tragedies which must get rid of the brutalities, the extravagance, the audacious mixture of farce and tragedy which was still attractive to the vulgar. He has, indeed, a kind of lurking regard for the rough vigour of the Shakespearian epoch; his patriotic prejudices pluck at him at intervals, and suggest that Marlborough's countrymen ought not quite to accept the yoke of the French Academy. When Ambrose Phillips produced the *Distrest Mother*—adapted from Racine—all Addison's little society was enthusiastic. Steele stated in the Prologue that the play was meant to combine French correctness with British force, and praised it in the *Spectator* because it was 'everywhere Nature.' The town, he pointed out, would be able to admire the passions 'within the rules of decency, honour, and good breeding.' The performance was soon followed by *Cato*, unquestionably, as Johnson still declares, 'the noblest production of Addison's genius.' It presents at any rate the closest conformity to the French model; and falls into comic results, as old Dennis pointed out, from the so-called Unity of Place, and consequent necessity of transacting all manner of affairs, love-making to Cato's daughter, and conspiring against Cato himself, in Cato's own hall. Such tragedy, however, refused to take root. Cato, as I think no one can deny, is a good specimen of Addison's style, but, except a few proverbial phrases, it is dead. The obvious cause, no doubt, is that the British public liked to see battle, murder, and sudden death, and, in spite of Addison's arguments, enjoyed a mixture of tragic and comic. Shakespeare, though not yet an idol, had still a hold upon the stage, and was beginning to be imitated by Rowe and to attract the attention of commentators. The sturdy Briton would not be seduced to the foreign model. The attempt to refine tragedy was as hopeless as the attempt to moralise comedy. This points to the process by which the Wit becomes 'artificial.' He has a profound conviction, surely not altogether wrong, that a tragedy ought to be a work of art. The artist must observe certain rules; though I need not ask whether he was right in thinking that these rules were represented by the accepted interpreters of the teaching of Nature. What he did not perceive was that another essential condition was absent; namely, that the tragic mood should correspond to his own 'nature.' The tragic art can, like other arts, only flourish when it embodies spontaneously the emotions and convictions of the spectators; when the dramatist is satisfying a genuine demand, and is himself ready to see in human life the conflict of great passions and the scene of impressive catastrophes. Then the theatre becomes naturally the mirror upon which the imagery can be projected. But the society to which Addison and his fellows belonged was a society of good, commonplace, sensible people, who were fighting each other by pamphlets instead of by swords; who played a game in which they staked not life and death but a comfortable competency; who did not even cut off the head of a fallen minister, who no longer believed in great statesmen of heroic proportions rising above the vulgar herd; and who had a very hearty contempt for romantic extravagance. A society in which common sense is regarded as the cardinal intellectual virtue does not naturally suggest the great tragic themes. Cato is obviously contrived, not inspired; and the dramatist is thinking of obeying the rules of good taste, instead of having them already incorporated in his thought. This comes out in one chief monument in the literary movement, I mean Pope's *Homer*. Pope, as we know, made himself independent by that performance. The method of publication is significant. He had no interest in the general sale, which was large enough to make his publisher's fortune. The publisher meanwhile supplied him gratuitously with the copies for which the subscribers paid him six guineas apiece. That means that he received a kind of commission from the upper class to execute the translation. The list of his subscribers seems to be almost a directory to the upper circle of the day; every person of quality has felt himself bound to promote so laudable an undertaking; the patron had been superseded by a kind of joint-stock body of collective patronage. The Duke of Buckingham, one of its accepted mouthpieces, had said in verse in his *Essay on Poetry* that if you once read Homer, everything else will be 'mean and poor.'

> 'Verse will seem prose; yet often in him look
> And you will hardly need another book.'

That was the correct profession of faith. Yet as a good many Wits found Greek an obstacle, a translation was needed. Chapman had become barbarous; Hobbes and Ogilvie were hopelessly flat; and Pope was therefore handsomely paid to produce a book which was to be the standard of the poetical taste. Pope was thus the chosen representative of the literary spirit. It is needless to point out that Pope's *Iliad* is not Homer's. That was admitted from the first. When we read in a speech of Agamemnon exhorting the Greeks to abandon the siege,

> 'Love, duty, safety summon us away;
> 'Tis Nature's voice, and Nature we obey,'

we hardly require to be told that we are not listening to Homer's Agamemnon but to an Agamemnon in a full-bottomed wig. Yet Pope's Homer had a success unparalleled by any other translation of profane poetry; for the rest of the century it was taken to be a masterpiece; it has been the book from which Byron and many clever lads first learned to enjoy what they at least took for Homer; and, as Mrs. Gallup has discovered, it was used by Bacon at the beginning of the seventeenth century, and by somebody at the beginning of the twentieth. That it has very high literary merits can, I think, be denied by no unprejudiced reader, but I have only to do with one point. Pope had the advantage—I take it to be an advantage—of having a certain style prescribed for him by the literary tradition inherited from Dryden. A certain diction and measure had to be adopted, and the language to be run into an accepted mould. The mould was no doubt conventional, and corresponded to a temporary phase of sentiment. Like the costume of the period, it strikes us now as 'artificial' because it was at the time so natural. It was worked out by the courtly and aristocratic class, and was fitted to give a certain dignity and lucidity, and to guard against mere greatness and triviality of utterance. At any rate it saved Pope from one enormous difficulty. The modern translator is aware that Homer lived a long time ago in a very different state of intellectual and social development, and yet feels bound to reproduce the impressions made upon the ancient Greek. The translator has to be an accurate scholar and to give the right shade of meaning for every phrase, while he has also to approximate to the metrical effect. The conclusion seems to be that the only language into which Homer could be adequately translated would be Greek, and that you must then use the words of the original. The actual result is that the translator is cramped by his fetters; that his use of archaic words savours of affectation, and that, at best, he has to emphasise the fact that his sentiments are fictitious. Pope had no trouble of that kind. He aims at giving something equivalent to Homer, not Homer himself, and therefore at something really practical. He has the same advantage as a man who accepts a living style of architecture or painting; he can exert all his powers of forcible expression in a form which will be thoroughly understood by his audience, and which saves him, though at a certain cost, from the difficulties of trying to reproduce the characteristics which are really incongruous.

There are disadvantages. In his time the learned M. Bossu was the accepted authority upon the canons of criticism. Buckingham says he had explained the 'mighty magic' of Homer. One doctrine of his was that an epic poet first thinks of a moral and then invents a fable to illustrate it. The theory struck Addison as a little overstated, but it is an exaggeration of the prevalent view. According to Pope Homer's great merit was his 'invention'—and by this he sometimes appears to imply that Homer had even invented the epic poem. Poetry was, it seems, at a 'low pitch' in Greece in Homer's time, as indeed were other arts and sciences. Homer, wishing to instruct his countrymen in all kinds of topics, devised the epic poem: made use of the popular mythology to supply what in the technical language was called his 'machinery'; converted the legends into philosophical allegory, and introduced 'strokes of knowledge from his whole circle of arts and sciences.' This 'circle' includes for example geography, rhetoric, and history; and the whole poem is intended to inculcate the political moral that many evils sprang from the want of union among the Greeks. Not a doubt of it! Homer was in the sphere of poetry what Lycurgus was supposed to be in the field of legislation. He had at a single bound created poetry and made it a vehicle of philosophy, politics, and ethics. Upon this showing the epic poem is a form of art which does not grow out of the historical conditions of the period; but it is a permanent form of art, as good for the eighteenth century as for the heroic age of Greece; it may be adopted as a model, only requiring certain additional ornaments and refinements to adapt it to the taste of a more enlightened period. Yet, at the same time, Pope could clearly perceive some of the absurd consequences of M. Bossu's view. He ridiculed that authority very keenly in the 'Recipe to make an Epic Poem' which first appeared in the *Guardian*, while he was at work upon his own translation. Bossu's rules, he says, will enable us to make epic poems without genius or reading; and he proceeds to show how you are to work your 'machines,' and introduce your allegories and descriptions, and extract your moral out of the fable at leisure, 'only making it sure that you strain it sufficiently.'

That was the point. The enlightened critic sees that the work of art embodies certain abstract rules; which may, and probably will—if he be a man of powerful intellectual power,—be rational, and suggest instructive canons. But, as Pope sees, it does not follow that the inverse process is feasible; that is, that you construct your poem simply by applying the rules. To be a good cricketer you must apply certain rules of dynamics; but it does not follow that a sound knowledge of dynamics will enable you to play good cricket. Pope sees that something more than an acceptance of M. Bossu's or Aristotle's canons is requisite for the writer of a good epic poem. The something more, according to him, appears to be learning and genius. It is certainly true that at least genius must be one requisite. But then, there is the further point. Will the epic poem, which was the product of certain remote social and intellectual conditions, serve to express the thoughts and emotions of a totally different age? Considering the difference between Achilles and Marlborough, or the bards of the heroic age and the wits who frequented clubs and coffee-houses under Queen Anne, it was at least important to ask whether Homer and Pope—taking them to be alike in genius—would not find it necessary to adopt radically different forms. That is for us so obvious a suggestion that one wonders at the tacit assumption of its irrelevance. Pope, indeed, by taking the *Iliad* for a framework, a ready-made fabric which he could embroider with his own tastes, managed to construct a singularly spirited work, full of good rhetoric and not infrequently rising to real poetical excellence. But it did not follow that an original production on the same lines would have been possible. Some years later, Young complained of Pope for being imitative, and said that if he had dared to be original, he might have produced a modern epic as good as the *Iliad* instead of a mere translation. That is not quite credible. Pope himself tried an epic poem too, which happily came to nothing; but a similar ambition led to such works as Glover's *Leonidas* and *The Epigoniad* of the Scottish Homer Wilkie. English poets as a rule seem to have suffered at some period of their lives from this malady and contemplated Arthuriads; but the constructional epic died, I take it, with Southey's respectable poems.

We may consider, then, that any literary form, the drama, the epic poem, the essay, and so forth, is comparable to a species in natural history. It has, one may say, a certain organic principle which determines the possible modes of development. But the line along which it will actually develop depends upon the character and constitution of the literary class which turns it to account, for the utterance of its own ideas; and depends also upon the correspondence of those ideas with the most vital and powerful intellectual currents of the time. The literary class of Queen Anne's day was admirably qualified for certain formations: the Wits leading the 'town,' and forming a small circle accepting certain canons of taste, could express with admirable clearness and honesty the judgment of bright common sense; the ideas which commend themselves to the man of the world, and to a rationalism which was the embodiment of common sense. They produced a literature, which in virtue of its sincerity and harmonious development within certain limits could pass for some time as a golden age. The aversion to pedantry limited its capacity for the highest poetical creation, and made the imagination subservient to the prosaic understanding. The comedy had come to adapt itself to the tastes of the class which, instead of representing the national movement, was composed of the more disreputable part of the town. The society unable to develop it in the direction of refinement left it to second-rate writers. It became enervated instead of elevated. The epic and the tragic poetry, ceasing to reflect the really powerful impulses of the day, were left to the connoisseur and dilettante man of taste, and though they could write with force and dignity when renovating or imitating older masterpieces, such literature became effete and hopelessly artificial. It was at best a display of technical skill, and could not correspond to the strongest passions and conditions of the time. The invention of the periodical essay, meanwhile, indicated what was a condition of permanent vitality. There, at least, the Wit was appealing to a wide and growing circle of readers, and could utter the real living thoughts and impulses of the time. The problem for the coming period was therefore marked out. The man of letters had to develop a living literature by becoming a representative of the ideas which really interested the whole cultivated classes, instead of writing merely for the exquisite critic, or still less for the regenerating and obnoxious section of society. That indeed, I take it, is the general problem of literature; but I shall have to trace the way in which its solution was attempted in the next period.

III

(1714-1739)

The death of Queen Anne opens a new period in the history of literature and of politics. Under the first Georges we are in the very heart of the eighteenth century; the century, as its enemies used to say, of coarse utilitarian aims, of religious indifference and political corruption; or, as I prefer to say, the century of sound common sense and growing toleration, and of steady social and industrial development.

To us, to me at least, it presents something pleasant in retrospect. There were then no troublesome people with philanthropic or political or religious nostrums, proposing to turn the world upside down and introduce an impromptu millennium. The history of periods when people were cutting each other's throats for creeds is no doubt more exciting; but we, who profess toleration, ought surely to remember that you cannot have martyrs without bigots and persecutors ; and that fanaticism, though it may have its heroic aspects, has also a very ugly side to it. At any rate, we who come after a century of revolutionary changes, and are often told that the whole order of things may be upset by some social earthquake, look back with regret to the days of quiet solid progress, when everything seemed to have settled down to a quiet, stable equilibrium. Wealth and comfort were growing—surely no bad things ; and John Bull—he had just received that name from Arbuthnot—was waxing fat and complacently contemplating his own admirable qualities. It is the period of the composition of 'Rule Britannia' and 'The Roast Beef of Old England,' and of the settled belief that your lusty, cudgel-playing, beer-drinking Briton was worth three of the slaves who ate frogs and wore wooden shoes across the Channel. The British constitution was the embodiment of perfect wisdom, and, as such, was entitled to be the dread and envy of the world. To the political historian it is the era of Walpole ; the huge mass of solid common sense, who combined the qualities of the sturdy country squire and the thorough man of business ; whose great aim was to preserve the peace ; to keep the country as much as might be out of the continental troubles which it did not understand, and in which it had no concern ; and to carry on business upon sound commercial principles. It is of course undeniable that his rule not only meant regard for the solid material interests of the country, but too often appealed to the interests of the ruling class. Philosophical historians who deal with the might-have-been may argue that a man of higher character might have worked by better means and have done something to purify the political atmosphere. Walpole was not in advance of his day ; but it is at least too clear to need any exposition that under the circumstances corruption was inevitable. When the House of Commons was the centre of political authority, when so many boroughs were virtually private property, when men were not stirred to the deeper issues by any great constitutional struggle —party government had to be carried on by methods which involved various degrees of jobbery and bribery. The disease was certainly not peculiar to Walpole's age ; though perhaps the symptoms were more obvious and avowed more bluntly than usual. As Walpole's masterful ways drove his old allies into opposition, they denounced the system and himself; but unfortunately although they claimed to be patriots and patterns of political virtue, they were made pretty much of the same materials as the arch-corrupter. When the 'moneyed men,' upon whom he had relied, came to be in favour of a warlike policy and were roused by the story of Captain Jenkins' ear, Walpole fell, but no reign of purity followed. The growing dissatisfaction, however, with the Walpolean system implied some very serious conditions, and the cry against corruption, in which nearly all the leading writers of the time joined, had a very serious significance in literature and in the growth of public opinion.

First, however, let me glance at the change as it immediately affected the literary organ. The old club and coffee-house society broke up with remarkable rapidity. While Oxford was sent to the Tower, and Bolingbroke escaped to France, Swift retired to Dublin, and Prior, after being imprisoned, passed the remainder of his life in retirement. Pope settled down to translating Homer, and took up his abode at Twickenham, outside the exciting and noisy London world in which the poor invalid had been jostled. Addison soared into the loftier regions of politics and married his Countess, and ceased to preside at Buttons'. Steele held on for a time, but in declining prosperity and diminished literary activity, till his retirement to Wales. No one appeared to fill the gaps thus made in the ranks either of the Whigs' or the Tories' section of literature. The change was obviously connected with the systematic development of the party system. Swift bitterly denounced Walpole for his indifference to literature! 'Bob the poet's foe' was guided by other motives in disposing of his patronage. Places in the Customs were no longer to be given to writers of plays or complimentary epistles in verse, or even to promising young politicians, but to members of parliament or the constituents in whom they were interested. The placemen, who were denounced as one of the great abuses of the time, were rewarded for voting power not for literary merit. The patron, therefore, was disappearing; though one or two authors, such as Congreve and Gay, might be still petted by the nobility; and Young somehow got a pension out of Walpole, probably through Bubb Dodington, the very questionable parson who still wished to be a Mæcenas. Meanwhile there was a compensation. The bookseller was beginning to supersede the patron. Tonson and Lintot were making fortunes; the first Longman was founding the famous firm which still flourishes; and the career of the disreputable and piratical Curll shows that at least the demand for miscellaneous literature was growing. The anecdotes of the misery of authors, of the translators who lay three in a bed in Curll's garret, of Samuel Boyse, who had reduced his clothes to a single blanket, and Savage sleeping on a bulk, are sometimes adduced to show that literature was then specially depressed. But there never was a time when authors of dissolute habits were not on the brink of starvation, and the authorities of the Literary Fund could give us contemporary illustrations of the fact. The real inference is, I take it, that the demand which was springing up attracted a great many impecunious persons, who became the drudges of the rising class of booksellers. No doubt the journalist was often in a degrading position. The press was active in all political struggles. The great men, Walpole, Bolingbroke, and Pulteney, wrote pamphlets or contributed papers to the *Craftsman*, while they employed inferior scribes to do the drudgery. Walpole paid large sums to the 'Gazetters,' whom Pope denounces; and men like Amherst of the *Craftsman* or Gordon of the *Independent Whig*, carried on the ordinary warfare. The author by profession was beginning to be recognised. Thomson and Mallet came up from Scotland during this period to throw themselves upon literature; Ralph, friend of Franklin and collaborator of Fielding, came from New England; and Johnson was attracted from the country to become a contributor to the *Gentleman's Magazine*, started by Cave in 1731—an event which marked a new development of periodical literature. Though no one would then advise a young man who could do anything else to trust to authorship (it would be rash to give such advice now) the new career was being opened. There were hack authors of all varieties. The successful playwright gained a real prize in the lottery; and translations, satires, and essays on the *Spectator* model enabled the poor drudge to make both ends meet, though too often in bondage to his employer to be, as I take it, better off than in the previous period, when the choice lay between risking the pillory and selling yourself as a spy.

Before considering the effect produced under the changed conditions, I must note briefly the intellectual position. The period was that of the culmination of the deist controversy. In the previous period the rationalism of which Locke was the mouthpiece represented the dominant tendency. It was generally held on all sides that there was a religion of nature, capable of purely rational demonstration. The problem remained as to its relation to the revealed religion and the established creed. Locke himself was a sincere Christian, though he reduced the dogmatic element to a minimum. Some of his disciples, however, became freethinkers in the technical sense, and held that revelation was needless, and that in point of fact no supernatural revelation had been made. The orthodox, on the other hand, while admitting or declaring that faith should be founded on reason, and that reason could establish a 'religion of nature,' admitted in various ways that a supernatural revelation was an essential corollary or a useful addition to the simple rational doctrine. The controversies which arose upon this issue, after being carried on very vigorously for a time, caused less interest as time went on, and were beginning to die out at the end of this period. It is often said in explanation that deism or the religion of nature, as then understood, was too vague and colourless a system to have any strong vitality. It faded into a few abstract logical propositions which had no relation to fact, and led to the optimistic formula, 'Whatever is, is right,' which could in the long-run satisfy no one with any strong perception of the darker elements of the world and human nature. This view may be emphasised by the most remarkable writings of the period. Butler's *Analogy* (1736) has been regarded by many even of his strongest opponents as triumphant against the deistical optimism, and certainly emphasises the side of things to which that optimism is blind. Hume's *Treatise of Human Nature*, at the end of the period (1739), uttered the sceptical revolution which destroys the base of the deistical system. Another writer is notable: William Law's *Serious Call* is one of the books which has made a turning-point in many men's lives. It specially affected Samuel Johnson and John Wesley, and many of those who sympathised more or less with Wesley's movement. Law was driven by his sense of the aspects of the rationalist theories to adopt a different position. He became a follower of Behmen, and his mysticism ended by repelling the thoroughly practical Wesley, as indeed mysticism in general seems to be uncongenial to the

English mind. Law's position shows a difficulty which was felt by others. It means that while he holds that religion must be in the highest sense 'reasonable' it cannot be (as another author put it) 'founded upon argument.' Faith must be identified with the inner light, the direct voice of God to man, which appeals to the soul, and is not built upon syllogisms or allowed to depend upon the result of historical criticism. This view, I need hardly say, is opposed to the whole rationalist theory, whether of the deist or the orthodox variety: it was so opposed that it could find scarcely any sympathy at the time; and for that reason it indicates one characteristic of the contemporary thought. To omit the mystical element is to be cold and unsatisfactory in religious philosophy, and to be radically prosaic and unpoetical in the sphere of literature. Englishmen could never become mystics in the technical sense, but they were beginning to be discontented with the bare logical system of the religion of nature. They were ready for some utterance of the emotional and imaginative element in religion and philosophy which was left out of account by the wits and rationalists. I do not myself believe that the intellectual weakness of abstract deism gives a sufficient explanation of its decay. In fact, as accepted by Rousseau and by some of his English followers, it could ally itself with the ardent revolutionary enthusiasm which was to be the marked peculiarity of the latter part of the century. We must add another consideration. Locke and his contemporaries had laid down political and religious principles which, if logically developed, would lead to the revolutionary doctrines of 1789. They did not develop them, and mainly, I take it, because the practical application excited no strong feeling. The spark did not find fuel ready to be lighted. The political and social conditions supply a sufficient explanation of the indifference. People were practically content with the existing order in Church and State. The deist controversies did not reach the enormous majority of the nation, who went quietly about their business in the old paths. The orthodox themselves were so rationalistic in principle that the whole discussion seemed to turn upon non-essential points. But moreover the Church was so thoroughly subordinated to the laity; it was so much a part of the regular comfortable system of things; so little able or inclined to set up as an independent power claiming special authority and enforcing discipline, that it excited no hostility. Parson and squire were part of the regular system which could not be attacked without upsetting the whole system; and there was as yet no general discontent with that system, or, indeed, any disposition whatever to reconstruct the machinery which was working so quietly and so thoroughly in accordance with the dumb instincts of the overwhelming majority.

Now let us pass to the literary manifestation of this order. The literary society, as it existed under Queen Anne, had been broken up; two or three of the men who had already made their mark continued their activity, especially Pope and Swift. Swift, however, was living apart from the world, though he was still to come to the front on more than one remarkable occasion. Pope, meanwhile, became the acknowledged dictator. The literary movement may be called after Pope, as distinctly as the political after Walpole. He established his dynasty so thoroughly that in later days the attempt to upset him was regarded as a daring revolution. What was Pope? Poet or not, for his title to the name has been disputed, he had one power or weakness in which he has scarcely been rivalled. No writer, that is, reflects so clearly and completely the spirit of his own day. His want of originality means the extreme and even morbid sensibility which enabled him to give the fullest utterance to the ideas of his class, and of the nation, so far as the nation was really represented by the class. But the literary class was going through a process of differentiation, as the alliance of authors and statesmen broke up. Pope represents mainly the aristocratic movement. He had become independent—a fact of which he was a little too proud—and moved on the most familiar terms with the great men of the age. The Tory leaders were, of course, his special friends; but in later days he became a friend of Frederick, Prince of Wales, and of the politicians who broke off from Walpole; while even with Walpole he was on terms of civility. His poems give a long catalogue of the great men of whose intimacy he was so proud. Besides Bolingbroke, his 'guide, philosopher, and friend,' he counts up nearly all the great men of his time. Somers and Halifax, and Granville and Congreve, Oxford and Atterbury, who had encouraged his first efforts; Pulteney, Chesterfield, Argyll, Wyndham, Cobham,

Bathurst, Peterborough, Queensberry, who had become friends in later years, receive the delicate compliments which imply his excusable pride in their alliance. Pope, therefore, may be considered from one point of view as the authorised interpreter of the upper circle, which then took itself to embody the highest cultivation of the nation. We may appreciate Pope's poetry by comparing it with an independent manifestation of their morality. The most explicit summary of the general tone of the class-morality may, I think, be gathered from Chesterfield's *Letters*. Though written at a later period, they sum up the lesson he has imbibed from his experience at this time. Chesterfield was no mere fribble or rake. He was a singularly shrewd, impartial observer of life, who had studied men at first hand as well as from books. His letters deal with the problem: What are the conditions of success in public life? He treats it in the method of Machiavelli; that is to say, he inquires what actually succeeds, not what ought to succeed. An answer to that question given by a man of great ability is always worth studying. Even if it should appear that success in this world is not always won by virtue, the fact should be recognised, though we should get rid of the conclusion that virtue, when an encumbrance to success, should be discarded. Chesterfield's answer, however, is not simply cynical. His pupil is to study men and politics thoroughly; to know the constitutions of all European states, to read the history of modern times so far as it has a bearing upon business; to be thoroughly well informed as to the aims of kings and courts; to understand financial and diplomatic movements; briefly, as far as was then possible, to be an incarnate blue-book. He was to study literature and appreciate art, though he was carefully to avoid the excess which makes the pedant or the virtuoso. He was to cultivate a good style in writing and speaking, and even to learn German. Chesterfield's prophecy of a revolution in France (though, I fancy, a little overpraised) shows at least that he was a serious observer of political phenomena. But besides these solid attainments, the pupil, we know, is to study the Graces. The excessive insistence upon this is partly due to the peculiarities of his hearer and his own quaint illusion that the way to put a man at his ease is to be constantly insisting upon his hopeless awkwardness. The theory is pushed to excess when he says that Marlborough and Pitt succeeded by the Graces, not by supreme business capacity or force of character; and argues from recent examples that a fool may succeed by dint of good manners, while a man of ability without them must be a failure. The exaggeration illustrates the position. The game of politics, that is, has become mainly personal. The diplomatist must succeed by making himself popular in courts, and the politician by winning popularity in the House of Commons. Social success—that is, the power of making oneself agreeable to the ruling class—is the essential pre-condition to all other success. The statesman does not make himself known as the advocate of great principles when no great principles are at stake, and the ablest man of business cannot turn his abilities to account unless he commends himself to employers who themselves are too good and great to be bothered with accounts. You must first of all be acceptable to your environment; and the environment means the upper ten thousand who virtually govern the world. The social qualities, therefore, come into the foreground. Undoubtedly this implies a cynical tone. You can't respect the victims of your cajolery. Chesterfield's favourite author is Rochefoucauld of whom (not the Bible) his son is to read a chapter every day. Men, that is, are selfish. Happily also they are silly, and can be flattered into helping you, little as they may care for you. 'Wriggle yourself into power' he says more than once. That is especially true of women, of whom he always speaks with the true aristocratic contempt. A man of sense will humour them and flatter them; he will never consult them seriously, nor really trust them, but he will make them believe that he does both. They are invaluable as tools, though contemptible in themselves. This, of course, represents the tone too characteristic of the epicurean British nobleman. Yet with all this cynicism, Chesterfield's morality is perfectly genuine in its way. He has the sense of honour and the patriotic feeling of his class. He has the good nature which is compatible with, and even congenial to, a certain cynicism. He is said to have achieved the very unusual success of being an admirable Lord-Lieutenant of Ireland. In fact he had the intellectual vigour which implies a real desire for good administration, less perhaps from purely philanthropic motives than from respect for efficiency.

'For forms of government let fools contest
Whate'er is best administered, is best,'

says Pope, and that was Chesterfield's view. Like Frederick of Prussia, whom he admires above all rulers, he might not be over-scrupulous in his policy, but wishes the machinery for which he is responsible to be in thoroughly good working order. He most thoroughly sees the folly, if he does not sufficiently despise the motives, of the lower order of politicians to whom bribery and corruption represented the only political forces worth notice. In practice he might be forced to use such men, but he sees them to be contemptible, and appreciates the mischiefs resulting from their rule.

The development of this morality in the aristocratic class, which was still predominant although the growing importance of the House of Commons was tending to shift the centre of political gravity to a lower point, is, I think, sufficiently intelligible to be taken for granted. Pope, I have said, represents the literary version. The problem, then, is how this view of life is to be embodied in poetry. One answer is the *Essay on Man*, in which Pope versified the deism which he learned from Bolingbroke, and which was characteristic of the upper circle generally. I need not speak of its shortcomings; didactic poetry of that kind is dreary enough, and the smart couplets often offend one's taste. I may say that here and there Pope manages to be really impressive, and to utter sentiments which really ennobled the deist creed; the aversion to narrow superstition; to the bigotry which 'dealt damnation round the land'; and the conviction that the true religion must correspond to a cosmopolitan humanity. I remember hearing Carlyle quote with admiration the Universal Prayer—

> 'Father of all, in every age,
> In every clime adored,
> By Saint, by Savage, and by Sage,
> Jehovah, Jove, or Lord,'

and it is the worthy utterance of one good legacy which the deist bequeathed to posterity. Pope himself was alarmed when he discovered that he had slipped unawares into heterodoxy. His creed was not congenial to the average mind, though it was to that of his immediate circle. Meanwhile, his most characteristic and successful work was of a different order. The answer, in fact, to the problem which I have just stated, is that the only kind of poetry that was congenial to his environment was satire—if satire can be called poetry. Pope's satires, the 'Epistle to Arbuthnot,' the 'Epilogue,' and some of the 'Imitations of Horace,' represent his best and most lasting achievement. There he gives the fullest expression to the general sentiment in the most appropriate form. His singular command of language, and, within his own limits, of versification, was turned to account by conscientious and unceasing labour in polishing his style. Particular passages, like the famous satire upon Addison, have been slowly elaborated; he has brooded over them for years; and, if the result of such methods is sometimes a mosaic rather than a continuous current of discourse, the extraordinary brilliance of some passages has made them permanently interesting and enriched our literature with many proverbial phrases. The art was naturally cultivated and its results appreciated in the circle formed by such men as Congreve, Bolingbroke, and Chesterfield and the like, by whom witty conversation was cultivated as a fine art. Chesterfield tells us that he never spoke without trying to express himself as well as possible; and Pope carries out the principle in his poetry. The thorough polish has preserved the numerous phrases, still familiar, which have survived the general neglect of his work. Pope indeed manages to introduce genuine poetry, as in his famous compliments or his passage about his mother, in which we feel that he is really speaking from his heart. But no doubt Atterbury gave him judicious (if not very Christian) advice, when he told him to stick to the vein of the Addison verses. The main topic of the satires is a denunciation of an age when, as he puts it,

> 'Not to be corrupted is the shame.'

He ascribes his own indignation to the 'strong antipathy of good to bad,' which is a satisfactory explanation to himself. But he was still interpreting the general sentiment and expressing the general discontent caused by the Walpole system. His friends, Bolingbroke and Wyndham, and the whole opposition, partially recruited from Walpole's supporters, were insisting upon the same theme. If, as I have said, some of them were really sincere in recognising the evil, and, like Bolingbroke in the *Patriot King*, trying to ascertain its source—we are troubled in this even by the doubt as to whether they objected to corruption or only to the corrupt influence of their antagonists. But Pope, as a poet, living outside the political circle, can take the denunciations quite seriously and be not only pointed but really dignified. He sincerely believes that vice can be seriously discouraged by lashing at it with epigrams. So far, he represented a general feeling of the literary class, explained in various ways by such men as Thomson, Fielding, Glover, and Johnson, who were, from very different points of view, in opposition to Walpole. Satire can only flourish under some such conditions as then existed. It supposes, among other things, the existence of a small cultivated class, which will fully appreciate the personalities, the dexterity of insinuation, and the cutting sarcasm which gives the spice to much of Pope's satire. Young, a singularly clever writer, was eclipsed by Pope because he kept to denoting general types and was not intimate with the actors on the social stage. Johnson, still more of an outsider, wrote a most effective and sonorous poem with the help of Juvenal; but it becomes a moral disquisition upon human nature which has not the special sting and sparkle of Pope. No later satirist has approached Pope, and the art has now become obsolete, or is adopted merely as a literary amusement. One obvious reason is the absence of the peculiar social backing which composed Pope's audience and supplied him with his readers.

The growing sense that there was something wrong about the political system which Pope turned to account was significant of coming changes. The impression that the evil was entirely due to Walpole personally was one of the natural illusions of party warfare, and the disease was not extirpated when the supposed cause was removed. The most memorable embodiment of the sentiment was Swift. The concentrated scorn of corruption in the *Drapier's Letters* was followed by the intense misanthropy of *Gulliver's Travels*. The singular way in which Swift blends personal aversion with political conviction, and the strange humour which conceals the misanthropist under a superficial playfulness, veils to some extent his real aim. But Swift showed with unequalled power and in an exaggerated form the conviction that there was something wrong in the social order, which was suggested by the conditions of the time and was to bear fruit in later days. Satire, however, is by its nature negative; it does not present a positive ideal, and tends to degenerate into mere hopeless pessimism. Lofty poetry can only spring from some inner positive enthusiasm.

I turn to another characteristic of the literary movement. I have called attention to the fact that while the Queen Anne writers were never tired of appealing to nature, they came to be considered as prematurely 'artificial.' The commonest meaning of 'natural' is that in which it is identified with 'normal.' We call a thing natural when its existence appears to us to be a matter of course, which again may simply mean that we are so accustomed to certain conditions that we do not remember that they are really exceptional. We take ourselves with all our peculiarities to be the 'natural' type or standard. An English traveller in France remarked that it was unnatural for soldiers to be dressed in blue; and then, remembering certain British cases, added, 'except, indeed, for the Artillery or the Blue Horse.' The English model, with all its variations, appeared to him to be ordained by Nature. This unconscious method of usurping a general name so as to cover a general meaning produces many fallacies. In any case, however, it was of the essence of Pope's doctrine that we should, as he puts its, 'Look through Nature up to Nature's God.' God, that is, is known through Nature, if it would not be more correct to say that God and Nature are identical. This Nature often means the world as not modified by human action, and therefore sharing the divine workmanship unspoilt by man's interference. Thus in the common phrase, the 'love of Nature' is generally taken to mean the love of natural scenery, of sea and sky and mountains, which are not altered or alterable by any human art. Yet it is said the want of any such love describes one of the most obvious deficiencies in Pope's poetry, of which Wordsworth so often complained. His famous preface asserts the complete absence of any imagery from Nature in the writings of the time. It was, however, at the period of which I am speaking that a change was taking place which was worth considering.

One cause is obvious. The Wit utters the voice of the town. He agreed with the gentleman who preferred the smell of a flambeau in St. James Street to any abundance of violet and sweetbriar. But, as communications improved between town and country, the separation between the taste of classes became less marked. The great nobleman had always been in part an exalted squire, and had a taste for field-sports as well as for the opera. Bolingbroke and Walpole are both instances in point. Sir Roger de Coverley came up to town more frequently than his ancestors, but the *Spectator* recorded his visitsas those of a simple rustic. After the peace, the country gentleman begins regularly to visit the Continent. The 'grand tour' mostly common in the preceding century becomes a normal fact of the education of the upper classes. The foundation of the Dilettante Club in 1734 marks the change. The qualifications, says Horace Walpole, were drunkenness and a visit to Italy. The founders of it seem to have been jovial young men who had met each other abroad, where, with obsequious tutors and out of sight of domestic authority, they often learned some very queer lessons. But many of them learned more, and by degrees the Dilettante Club took not only to encouraging the opera in England, but to making really valuable archæological researches in Greece and elsewhere. The intelligent youth had great opportunities of mixing in the best foreign society, and began to bring home the pictures which adorn so many English country houses ; to talk about the 'correggiosity of Correggio'; and in due time to patronise Reynolds and Gainsborough. The traveller began to take some interest even in the Alps, wrote stanzas to the 'Grande Chartreuse,' admired Salvator Rosa, and even visited Chamonix. Another characteristic change is more to the present purpose. A conspicuous mark of the time was a growing taste for gardening. The taste has, I suppose, existed ever since our ancestors were turned out of the Garden of Eden. Milton's description of that place of residence, and Bacon's famous essay, and Cowley's poems addressed to the great authority Evelyn, and most of all perhaps Maxwell's inimitable description of the very essence of garden, may remind us that it flourished in the seventeenth century. It is needless to say in Oxford how beautiful an old-fashioned garden might be. But at this time a change was taking place in the canons of taste. Temple in a well-known essay had praised the old-fashioned garden and had remarked how the regularity of English plantations seemed ridiculous to—of all people in the world—the Chinese. By the middle of the eighteenth century there had been what is called a 'reaction,' and the English garden, which was called 'natural,' was famous and often imitated in France. It is curious to remark how closely this taste was associated with the group of friends whom Pope has celebrated. The first, for example, of the four 'Moral Epistles,' is addressed to Cobham, who laid out the famous garden at Stowe, in which 'Capability Brown,' the most popular landscape gardener of the century, was brought up; the third is addressed to Bathurst, an enthusiastic gardener, who had shown his skill at his seat of Richings near Colnbrook; and the fourth to Burlington, whose house and gardens at Chiswick were laid out by Kent, the famous landscape gardener and architect—Brown's predecessor. In the same epistle Pope ridicules the formality of Chandos' grounds at Canons. A description of his own garden includes the familiar lines

> 'Here St. John mingles with my friendly bowl
> The feast of reason and the flow of soul,
> And he (Peterborough) whose lightning pierced the
> Iberian lines
> Now forms my quincunx and now ranks my vines,
> Or tames the genius of the stubborn plain
> Almost as quickly as he conquered Spain.'

Pope's own garden was itself a model. 'Pope,' says Horace Walpole, 'had twisted and twirled and rhymed and harmonised his little five acres till it appeared two or three sweet little lawns opening and opening beyond one another, and the whole surrounded with thick impenetrable woods.' The taste grew as the century advanced. Now one impulse towards the new style is said to have come from articles in the *Spectator* by Addison and in the *Guardian* by Pope, ridiculing the old-fashioned mode of clipping trees, and so forth. Nature, say both, is superior to art, and the man of genius, as Pope puts it, is the first to perceive that all art consists of 'imitation and study of nature.' Horace Walpole in his essay upon gardening remarks a point which may symbolise the principle. The modern style, he says, sprang from the invention of the ha-ha by Bridgeman, one of the first landscape gardeners. The 'ha-ha' meant that the garden, instead of being enclosed by a wall, was laid out so as to harmonise with the surrounding country, from which it was only separated by an invisible fence. That is the answer to the problem; is it not a solecism for a lover of gardens to prefer nature to art? A garden is essentially a product of art? and supplants the moor and desert made by unassisted nature. The love of Nature as understood in a later period, by

Byron for example, went to this extreme, in words at least, and becomes misanthropical in admiring the savage for its own sake. But the landscape gardener only meant that his art must be in some sense subordinate to nature; that he must not shut out the wider scenery but include it in his designs. He was apt to look upon mountains as a background to parks, as Telford thought that rivers were created to supply canals. The excellent Gilpin, who became an expounder of what he calls 'the theory of the picturesque,' travelled on the Wye in the same year as Gray; and amusingly criticises nature from this point of view. Nature, he says, works in a cold and singular style of composition, but has the merit of never falling into 'mannerism.' Nature, that is, is a sublime landscape gardener whose work has to be accepted, and to whom the gardener must accommodate himself. A quaint instance of this theory may be found in the lecture which Henry Tilney in *Mansfield Park* delivers to Catherine Morland. In Horace Walpole's theory, the evolution of the ha-ha, means that man and nature, the landowner and the country, are gradually forming an alliance, and it comes to the same thing whether one or the other assimilates his opposite.

Briefly, this means one process by which the so-called love of nature was growing; it meant better roads and inns; the gradual reflux of town into country; and the growing sense already expressed by Cowley and Marvell, that overcrowded centres of population have their inconveniences, and that the citizen should have his periods of communion with unsophisticated nature. Squire and Wit are each learning to appreciate each other's tastes. The tourist is developed, and begins, as Gibbon tells us, to 'view the glaciers' now that he can view them without personal inconvenience. This, again, suggests that there is nothing radically new in the so-called love of nature. Any number of poets from Chaucer downwards may be cited to show that men were never insensible to natural beauty of scenery; to the outburst of spring, or the bloom of flowers, or the splendours of storms and sunsets. The indifference to nature of the Pope school was, so far, the temporary complacency of the new population focused in the metropolitan area in their own enlightenment and their contempt for the outside rustic. The love of field-sports was as strong as ever in the squire, and as soon as he began to receive some of the intellectual irradiation from the town Wit, he began to express the emotions which never found clearer utterance than in Walton's *Compleat Angler*. But there is a characteristic difference. With the old poets nature is in the background; it supplies the scenery for human action and is not itself consciously the object; they deal with concrete facts, with the delight of sport or rustic amusements: and they embody their feelings in the old conventions; they converse with imaginary shepherds: with Robin Hood or allegorical knights in romantic forests, who represent a love of nature but introduce description only as a set-off to the actors in masques or festivals. In Pope's time we have the abstract or metaphysical deity Nature, who can be worshipped with a distinct appreciation. The conventions have become obsolete, and if used at all, the poet himself is laughing in his sleeve. The serious aim of the poet is to give a philosophy of human nature; and the mere description of natural objects strikes him as silly unless tacked to a moral. Who could take offence, asks Pope, referring to his earlier poems, 'when pure description held the place of sense'? The poet, that is, who wishes to be 'sensible' above all, cannot condescend to give mere catalogues of trees and rivers and mountains. Nature, however, is beginning to put in a claim for attention, even in the sense in which Nature means the material world. In one sense this is a natural corollary from the philosophy of the time and of that religion of nature which it implied. Pope himself gives one version of it in the *Essay on Man*; and can expatiate eloquently upon the stars and upon the animal world. But the poem itself is essentially constructed out of a philosophical theory too purely argumentative to lend itself easily to poetry. A different, though allied, way of dealing with the subject appears elsewhere. If Pope learned mainly from Bolingbroke, he was also influenced by Shaftesbury of the *Characteristics*. I note, but cannot here insist upon, Shaftesbury's peculiar philosophical position. He inherited to some extent the doctrine of the Cambridge Platonists and repudiated the sensationalist doctrine of Locke and the metaphysical method of Clarke. He had a marked influence on Hutcheson, Butler, and the common-sense philosophers of his day. For us, it is enough to say that he worships Nature but takes rather the æsthetic than the dialectical point of view. The Good, the True, and the Beautiful are all one, as he constantly insists, and the universe impresses us not as a set of mechanical contrivances but as an artistic embodiment of harmony. He therefore restores the universal element which is apt to pass out of sight in Pope's rhymed arguments. He indulges his philosophical enthusiasm in what he calls *The Moralists, a Rhapsody.* It culminates in a prose hymn to a 'glorious Nature, supremely fair and sovereignly good; all-loving and all-lovely, all divine,' which ends by a survey of the different climates, where even in the moonbeams and the shades of the forests we find intimations of the mysterious being who pervades the universe. A love of beauty was, in this sense, a thoroughly legitimate development of the 'Religion of Nature.' Akenside in his philosophical poem *The Pleasures of Imagination*, written a little later, professed himself to be a disciple of Shaftesbury, and his version supplied many quotations for Scottish professors of philosophy. Henry Brooke's *Universal Beauty*, a kind of appendix to Pope's essay, is upon the same theme, though he became rather mixed in physiological expositions, which suggested, it is said, Darwin's *Botanic Garden.* The religious sentiment embodied in his *Fool of Quality* charmed Wesley and was enthusiastically admired by Kingsley. Thomson, however, best illustrates this current of sentiment. The fine 'Hymn of Nature' appended to the *Seasons*, is precisely in the same vein as Shaftesbury's rhapsody. The descriptions of nature are supposed to suggest the commentary embodied in the hymn. He still describes the sea and sky and mountains with the more or less intention of preaching a sermon upon them. That is the justification of the 'pure description' which Pope condemned in principle, and which occupies the larger part of the poem. Thomson, when he wrote the sermons, was still fresh from Edinburgh and from Teviotdale. He had a real eye for scenery, and describes from observation. The English Wits had not, it seems, annexed Scotland, and Thomson had studied Milton and Spenser without being forced to look through Pope's spectacles. Still he cannot quite trust himself. He is still afraid, and not without reason, that pure description will fall into flat prose, and tries to 'raise his diction'—in the phrase of the day—by catching something of the Miltonic harmony and by speaking of fish as 'finny tribes' and birds as 'the feathered people.' The fact, however, that he could suspend his moralising to give realistic descriptions at full length, and that they became the most interesting parts of the poem, shows a growing interest in country life. The supremacy of the town Wit is no longer unquestioned; and there is an audience for the plain direct transcripts of natural objects for which the Wit had been too dignified and polished. Thomson had thus the merit of representing a growing sentiment—and yet he has not quite solved the problem. His philosophy is not quite fused with his observation. To make 'Nature' really interesting you must have a touch of Wordsworthian pantheism and of Shelley's 'pathetic fallacy.' Thomson's facts and his commentary lie in separate compartments. To him, apparently, the philosophy is more important than the simple description. His masterpiece was to be the didactic and now forgotten poem on *Liberty*. It gives an interesting application; for there already we have the sentiment which was to become more marked in later years. 'Liberty' crosses the Alps and they suggest a fine passage on the beauty of mountains. Nature has formed them as a rampart for the homely republics which worship 'plain Liberty'; and are free from the corruption typified by Walpole. That obviously is the germ of the true Rousseau version of Nature worship. On the whole, however, Nature, as interpreted by the author of 'Rule Britannia,' is still very well satisfied with the British Constitution and looks upon the Revolution of 1688 as the avatar of the true goddess. 'Nature,' that is, has not yet come to condemn civilisation in general as artificial and therefore corrupt. As in practice, a lover of Nature did not profess to prefer the wilderness to fields, and looked upon mountains rather as a background to the nobleman's park than as a shelter for republics ; so in politics it reflected no revolutionary tendency but rather included the true British system which has grown up under its protection. Nature has taken to lecturing, but she only became frankly revolutionary with Rousseau and misanthropic with Byron.

I must touch one more characteristic. Pope, I have said, represents the aristocratic development of literature. Meanwhile the purely plebeian society was growing, and the toe of the clown beginning to gall the kibe of the courtier. Pope's 'war with the dunces' was the historical symptom of this most important social development. The *Dunciad*, which, whatever its occasional merits, one cannot read without spasms both of disgust and moral disapproval, is the literary outcome. Pope's morbid sensibility perverts his morals till he accepts the worst of aristocratic prejudices and treats poverty as in itself criminal. It led him, too, to attack some worthy people, and among others the 'earless' Defoe. Defoe's position is most significant. A journalist of supreme ability, he had an abnormally keen eye for the interesting. No one could feel the pulse of his audience with greater quickness. He had already learned by inference that nothing interests the ordinary reader so much as a straightforward narrative of contemporary facts. He added the remark that it did not in the least matter whether the facts had or had not happened; and secondly, that it saved a great deal of trouble to make your facts instead of finding them. The result was the inimitable *Robinson Crusoe*, which was, in that sense, a simple application of journalistic methods, not a conscious attempt to create a new variety of novel. Alexander Selkirk had very little to tell about his remarkable experience; and so Defoe, instead of confining himself like the ordinary interviewer to facts, proceeded to tell a most circumstantial and elaborate lie—for which we are all grateful. He was doing far more than he meant. Defoe, as the most thorough type of the English class to which he belonged, could not do otherwise than make his creation a perfect embodiment of his own qualities. *Robinson Crusoe* became, we know, a favourite of Rousseau, and has supplied innumerable illustrations to writers on Political Economy. One reason is that Crusoe is the very incarnation of individualism: thrown entirely upon his own resources, he takes the position with indomitable pluck; adapts himself to the inevitable as quietly and sturdily as may be; makes himself thoroughly at home in a desert island, and, as soon as he meets a native, summarily annexes him, and makes him thoroughly useful. He comes up smiling after many years as if he had been all the time in a shop in Cheapside without a hair turned. This exemplary person not only embodies the type of middle class Briton but represents his most romantic aspirations. In those days the civilised world was still surrounded by the dim mysterious regions, where geographers placed elephants instead of towns, but where the adventurous Briton was beginning to push his way into strange native confines and to oust the wretched foreigner, Dutch, French, Spanish, and Portuguese, who had dared to anticipate him. Crusoe is the voice of the race which was to be stirred by the story of Jenkins' ear and lay the foundation of the Empire. Meanwhile, as a literary work, it showed most effectually the power of homely realism. There is no bother about dignity or attempt to reveal the eloquence of the polished Wit. It is precisely the plain downright English vernacular which is thoroughly intelligible to everybody who is capable of reading. The Wit, too, as Swift sufficiently proved, could be a consummate master of that kind of writing on occasion, and Gulliver probably showed something to Crusoe. But for us the interest is the development of a new class of readers, who won't bother about canons of taste or care for skill in working upon the old conventional methods, but can be profoundly interested in a straightforward narrative adapted to the simplest understandings. Pope's contempt for the dunces meant that the lower classes were the objects of supreme contempt to the aristocratic circle, whose culture they did not share. But Defoe was showing in a new sense of the word the advantage of an appeal to Nature; for the true life and vigour of the nation was coming to be embodied in the class which was spontaneously developing its own ideals and beginning to regard the culture of the upper circle as artificial in the objectionable sense. Outside the polished circle of wits we have the middle-class which is beginning to read, and will read, what it really likes without bothering about Aristotle or M. Bossu: as, in the other direction, the assimilation between town and country is incidentally suggesting a wider range of topics, and giving a new expression to conditions which had for some time been without expression.

IV

(1739-1763)

I AM now to speak of the quarter of a century which succeeded the fall of Walpole, and includes two singularly contrasted periods. Walpole's fall meant the accession to power of the heterogeneous body of statesmen whose virtuous indignation had been raised by his corrupt practices. Some of them, as Carteret, Pulteney, Chesterfield, were men of great ability; but, after a series of shifting combinations and personal intrigues, the final result was the triumph of the Pelhams—the grotesque Duke of Newcastle and his brother, who owed their success mainly to skill in the art of parliamentary management. The opposition had ousted Walpole by taking advantage of the dumb instinct which impelled us to go to war with Spain; and distracted by the interests of Hanover and the balance of power we had plunged into that complicated series of wars which lasted for some ten years, and passes all powers of the ordinary human intellect to understand or remember. For what particular reason Englishmen were fighting at Dettingen or Fontenoy or Lauffeld is a question which a man can only answer when he has been specially crammed for examination and his knowledge has not begun to ooze out; while the abnormal incapacity of our rulers was displayed at the attack upon Carthagena or during the Pretender's march into England. The history becomes a shifting chaos marked by no definite policy, and the ship of State is being steered at random as one or other of the competitors for rule manages to grasp the helm for a moment. Then after another period of aimless intrigues the nation seems to rouse itself; and finding at last a statesman who has a distinct purpose and can appeal to a great patriotic sentiment, takes the leading part in Europe, wins a series of victories, and lays the foundation of the British Empire in America and India. Under Walpole's rule the House of Commons had become definitely the dominant political body. The minister who could command it was master of the position. The higher aristocracy are still in possession of great influence, but they are ceasing to be the adequate representatives of the great political forces. They are in the comfortable position of having completely established their own privileges; and do not see any reason for extending privileges to others. Success depends upon personal intrigues among themselves and upon a proper manipulation of the Lower House which, though no overt constitutional change has taken place, is coming to be more decidedly influenced by the interests of the moneyed men and the growing middle classes. Pitt and Newcastle represent the two classes which are coming into distinct antagonism. Pitt's power rested upon the general national sentiment. 'You have taught me,' as George II. said to him, 'to look for the sense of my people in other places than the House of Commons.' The House of Commons, that is, should not derive its whole authority from the selfish interest of the borough-mongers but from the great outside current of patriotic sentiment and aspiration. But public opinion was not yet powerful enough to support the great minister without an alliance with the master of the small arts of intrigue. The general sentiments of discontent which had been raised by Walpole was therefore beginning to widen and deepen and to take a different form. The root of the evil, as people began to feel, was not in the individual Walpole but in the system which he represented. Brown's *Estimate* is often noticed in illustration. Brown convinced his readers, as Macaulay puts it, that they were a race of cowards and scoundrels, who richly deserved the fate in store for them of being speedily enslaved by their enemies ; and the prophecy was published (1757) on the eve of the most glorious war we had ever known. It represents also, as Macaulay observes, the indignation roused by the early failures of the war and the demand that Pitt should take the helm. Brown was a very clever, though not a very profound, writer. A similar and more remarkable utterance had been made some years before (1749) by the remarkable thinker, David Hartley. The world, he said, was in the most critical state ever known. He attributes the evil to the growth of infidelity in the upper classes ; their general immorality ; their sordid self-interest, which was almost the sole motive of action of the ministers ; the contempt for authority of all their superiors ; the worldly-mindedness of the clergy and the general carelessness as to education. These sentiments are not the mere platitudes, common to moralists in all ages. They are pointed and emphasised by the state of political and social life in the period. Besides the selfishness and want of principle of the upper classes, one fact upon which Hartley insists is sufficiently familiar. The Church it is obvious had been paralysed. It had no corporate activity; it was in thorough subjection to the aristocracy; the highest preferments were to be won by courting such men as Newcastle, and not by learning or by active discharge of duty; and the ordinary parson, though he might be thoroughly respectable and amiable, was dependant upon the squire as his superior upon the ministers. He took things easily enough to verify Hartley's remarks. We must infer from later history that a true diagnosis would not have been so melancholy as Hartley supposed. The nation was not corrupt at the core. It was full of energy; and rapidly developing in many directions. The upper classes, who had gained all they wanted, were comfortable and irresponsible; not yet seriously threatened by agitators; able to carry on a traffic in sinecures and pensions, and demoralised as every corporate body becomes demoralised which has no functions to discharge in proportion to capacities. The Church naturally shared the indolence of its rulers and patrons. Hartley exhorts the clergy to take an example from the energy of the Methodists instead of abusing them. Wesley had begun his remarkable missionary career in 1738, and the rapid growth of his following is a familiar proof on the one side of the indolence of the established authorities, and on the other of the strength of the demand for reform in classes to which he appealed. If, that is, the clergy were not up to their duties, Wesley's success shows that there was a strong sense of existing moral and social evils which only required an energetic leader to form a powerful organisation. I need not attempt to inquire into the causes of the Wesleyan and Evangelical movement, but must note one characteristic—it had not an intellectual but a sound moral origin. Wesley takes his creed for granted, and it was the creed, so far as they had one, of the masses of the nation. He is shocked by perjury, drunkenness, corruption, and so forth, but has not seriously to meet scepticism of the speculative variety. If Wesley did not, like the leader of another Oxford movement, feel bound to clear up the logical basis of his religious beliefs, he had of course to confront deism, but could set it down as a mere product of moral indifference. When Hartley, like Butler, speaks of the general unbelief of the day, he was no doubt correct within limits. In the upper social sphere the tone was sceptical. Not only Bolingbroke but such men as Chesterfield and Walpole were indifferent or contemptuous. They were prepared to go with Voltaire's development of the English rationalism. But the English sceptic of the upper classes was generally a Gallio. He had no desire to propagate his creed, still less to attack the Church, which was a valuable part of his property ; it never occurred to him that scepticism might lead to a political as well as an ecclesiastical revolution. Voltaire was not intentionally destructive in politics, whatever the real effect of his teaching ; but he was an avowed and bitter enemy of the Church and the orthodox creed. Hume, the great English sceptic, was not only a Tory in politics but had no desire to affect the popular belief. He could advise a clergyman to preach the ordinary doctrines, because it was paying far too great a compliment to the vulgar to be punctilious about speaking the truth to them. A similar indifference is characteristic of the whole position. The select classes were to be perfectly convinced that the accepted creed was superstitious; but they were not for that reason to attack it. To the statesman, as Gibbon was to point out, a creed is equally useful, true or false; and the English clergy, though bound to use orthodox language, were far too well in hand to be regarded as possible persecutors. Even in Scotland they made no serious attempt to suppress Hume; he had only to cover his opinions by some decent professions of belief. One symptom of the general state of mind is the dying out of the deist controversies. The one great divine, according to Brown's *Estimate*, was Warburton, the colossus, he says, who bestrides the world: and Warburton, whatever else he may have been, was certainly of all divines the one whose argument is most palpably fictitious, if not absolutely insincere. He marks, however, the tendency of the argument to become historical. Like a much acuter writer, Conyers Middleton, he is occupied with the curious problem: how do we reconcile the admission that miracles never happen with the belief that they once happened?—or are the two beliefs reconcilable? That means, is history continuous? But it also means that the problems of abstract theology were passing out of sight, and that speculation was turning to the historical and scientific problems. Hartley was expounding the association principle which became the main doctrine of the empirical school, and Hume was teaching ethics upon the same basis, and turning from speculation to political history. The main reason of this intellectual indifference was the social condition under which the philosophical theory found no strong current of political discontent with which to form an alliance. The middle classes, which are now growing in strength and influence, had been indifferent to the discussions going on above their heads. The more enlightened clergy had, of course, been engaged in the direct controversy, and had adopted a kind of mild common-sense rationalism which implied complete indifference to the dogmatic disputes of the preceding century. The Methodist movement produced a little revival of the Calvinist and Arminian controversy. But the beliefs of the great mass of the population were not materially affected: they held by sheer force of inertia to the old traditions, and still took themselves to be good orthodox Protestants, though they had been unconsciously more affected by the permeation of rationalism than they realised.

So much must be said, because the literary work was being more and more distinctly addressed to the middle class. The literary profession is now taking more of the modern form. Grub Street is rapidly becoming respectable, and its denizens—as Beauclerk said of Johnson when he got his pension—will be able to 'purge and live cleanly like gentlemen.' Johnson's incomparable letter (1755) rejecting Chesterfield's attempt to impose his patronage, is the familiar indication of the change. Johnson had been labouring in the employment of the booksellers, and always, unlike some more querulous authors, declares that they were fair and liberal patrons—though it is true that he had to knock down one of them with a folio. Other writers of less fame can turn an honest penny by providing popular literature of the heavier kind. There is a demand for 'useful information.' There was John Campbell, for example, the 'richest author,' said Johnson, who ever grazed 'the common of literature,' who contributed to the *Modern Universal History*, the *Biographica Britannica*, and wrote the *Lives of the Admirals* and the *Political Survey of Great Britain*, and innumerable historical and statistical works; and the queer adventurer Sir John Hill, who turned out book after book with marvellous rapidity and impudence, and is said to have really had some knowledge of botany. The industrious drudges and clever charlatans could make a respectable income. Smollett is a superior example, whose 'literary factory,' as it has been said, 'was in full swing' at this period, and who, besides his famous novels, was journalist, historian, and author of all work, and managed to keep himself afloat, though he also contrived to exceed his income and was supported by a number of inferior 'myrmidons' who helped to turn out his hack-work. He describes the author's position in a famous passage in *Humphry Clinker* (1756). Smollett also started the *Critical Review* in rivalry to the *Monthly Review*, begun by Griffiths a few years before (1749), and these two were for a long time the only precursors to the *Edinburgh Review*, and marked an advance upon the old *Gentleman's Magazine*. In other words, we have the beginning of a new tribunal or literary Star Chamber. The author has not to inquire what is said of his performances in the coffee-houses, where the Wits gathered under the presidency of

Addison or Swift. The professional critic has appeared who will make it his regular business to give an account of all new books, and though his reviews are still comparatively meagre and apt to be mere analyses, it is implied that a kind of public opinion is growing up which will decide upon his merits, and upon which his success or failure will depend. That means again that the readers to whom he is to appeal are mainly the middle class, who are not very highly cultivated, but who have at any rate reached the point of reading their newspaper and magazine regularly, and buy books enough to make it worth while to supply the growing demand. The nobleman has ceased to consider the patronage of authors as any part of his duty, and the tradition which made him consider writing poetry as a proper accomplishment is dying out. Since that time our aristocracy as such has been normally illiterate. Peers—Byron, for example—have occasionally written books; and more than one person of quality has, like Fox, kept up the interest in classical literature which he acquired at a public school, and added a charm to his parliamentary oratory. The great man, too, as I have said, could take his chance in political writing, and occasionally condescend to show his skill at an essay of the *Spectator* model. But a certain contempt for the professional writer is becoming characteristic, even of men like Horace Walpole, who have a real taste for literature. He is inclined to say, as Chesterfield put it in a famous speech, 'We, my lords, may thank Heaven that we have something better than our brains to depend upon.' As literature becomes more of a regular profession, your noble wishes to show his independence of anything like a commercial pursuit. Walpole can speak politely to men like Gibbon, and even to Hume, who have some claim to be gentlemen as well as authors; but he feels that he is condescending even to them, and has nothing but contemptuous aversion for a Johnson, whose claim to consideration certainly did not include any special refinement. Johnson and his circle had still an odour of Grub street, which is only to be kept at a distance more carefully because it is in a position of comparative independence. Meanwhile, the author himself holds by the authority of Addison and Pope. They, he still admits for the most part, represent the orthodox church; their work is still taken to be the perfection of art, and the canons which they have handed down have a prestige which makes any dissenter an object of suspicion. Yet as the audience has really changed, a certain change also makes itself felt in the substance and the form of the corresponding literature.

One remarkable book marks the opening of the period. The first part of Young's *Night Thoughts* appeared in 1742, and the poem at once acquired a popularity which lasted at least through the century. Young had been more or less associated with the Addison and Pope circles, in the later part of Queen Anne's reign. He had failed to obtain any satisfactory share of the patronage which came to some of his fellows. He is still a Wit till he has to take orders for a college living as the old Wits' circle is decaying. He tried with little success to get something by attaching himself to some questionable patrons who were induced to carry on the practice, and the want of due recognition left him to the end of his life as a man with a grievance. He had tried poetical epistles, and satires, and tragedies with undeniable success and had shown undeniable ability. Yet somehow or other he had not, one may say, emerged from the second class till in the *Night Thoughts* he opened a new vein which exactly met the contemporary taste. The success was no doubt due to some really brilliant qualities, but I need not here ask in what precise rank he should be placed, as an author or a moralist. His significance for us is simple. The *Night Thoughts*, as he tells us, was intended to supply an omission in Pope's *Essay on Man*. Pope's deistical position excluded any reference to revealed religion, to posthumous rewards and penalties, and expressed an optimistic philosophy which ignored the corruption of human nature. Young represents a partial revolt against the domination of the Pope circle. He had always been an outsider, and his life at Oxford had, you may perhaps hope, preserved his orthodoxy. He writes blank verse, though evidently the blank verse of a man accustomed to the 'heroic couplets'; he uses the conventional 'poetic diction'; he strains after epigrammatic point in the manner of Pope, and the greater part of his poem is an elaborate argumentation to prove the immortality of man—chiefly by the argument from astronomy. But though so far accepting the old method, his success in introducing a new element marks an important change. He is elaborately and deliberately pathetic; he is always thinking of death, and calling upon the readers to sympathise with his sorrows and accept his consolations. The world taken by itself is, he maintains, a huge lunatic asylum, and the most hideous of sights is a naked human heart. We are, indeed, to find sufficient consolation from the belief in immortality. How far Young was orthodox or logical or really edifying is a question with which I am not concerned. The appetite for this strain of melancholy reflection is characteristic. Blair's *Grave*, representing another version of the sentiment, appeared simultaneously and independently. Blair, like Thomson, living in Scotland, was outside the Pope circle of wit, and had studied the old English authors instead of Pope and Dryden. He negotiated for the publication of his poem through Watts and Doddridge, each of whom was an eminent interpreter of the religious sentiment of the middle classes. Both wrote hymns still popular, and Doddridge's *Rise and Progress of Religion in the Soul* has been a permanently valued manual. The Pope school had omitted religious considerations, and treated religion as a system of abstract philosophy. The new class of readers wants something more congenial to the teaching of their favourite ministers and chapels.

Young and Blair thoroughly suited them. Wesley admired Young's poem, and even proposed to bring out an edition. In his *Further Appeal to Men of Reason and Religion*, Wesley, like Brown and Hartley, draws up a striking indictment of the manners of the time. He denounces the liberty and effeminacy of the nobility; the wide-spread immorality; the chicanery of lawyers; the jobbery of charities; the stupid self-satisfaction of Englishmen; the brutality of the Army; the indolence and preferment humbug of the Church —the true cause, as he says, of the 'contempt for the clergy' which had become proverbial. His remedy of course is to be found in a revival of true religion. He accepts the general sentiment that the times are out of joint, though he would seek for a deeper cause than that which was recognised by the political satirist. While Young was weeping at Welwyn, James Hervey was meditating among the tombs in Devonshire, and soon afterwards gave utterance to the result in language inspired by very bad taste, but showing a love of nature and expressing the 'sentimentalism' which was then a new discovery. It is said to have eclipsed Law's *Serious Call*, which I have already mentioned as giving, in admirable literary form, the view of the contemporary world which naturally found favour with religious thinkers.

These symptoms indicate the tendencies of the rising class to which the author has mainly to address himself. It has ceased to be fully represented by the upper social stratum whose tastes are reflected by Pope. No distinct democratic sentiment had yet appeared; the aristocratic order was accepted as inevitable or natural; but there was a vague though growing sentiment that the rulers are selfish and corrupt. There is no strong sceptical or anti-religious sentiment; but a spreading conviction that the official pastors are scandalously careless in supplying the wants of their flocks. The philosophical and literary canons of the scholar and gentleman have become unsatisfactory; the vulgar do not care for the delicate finish appreciated by your Chesterfield and acquired in the conversations of polite society, and the indolent scepticism which leads to metaphysical expositions, and is not allied with any political or social passion, does not appeal to them. The popular books of the preceding generation had been the directly religious books: Baxter's *Saint's Rest*, and the *Pilgrim's Progress*—

despised by the polite but beloved by the popular class in spite of the critics; and among the dissenters such a work as Boston's *Fourfold State*, or in the Church, Law's *Serious Call.* Your polite author had ignored the devil, and he plays a part in human affairs which, as Carlyle pointed out in later days, cannot be permanently overlooked. The old horned and hoofed devil, indeed, for whom Defoe had still a weakness, shown in his *History of the Devil*, was becoming a little incredible; witchcraft was dying out, though Wesley still felt bound to profess some belief in it; and the old Calvinistic dogmatism, though it could produce a certain amount of controversy among the Methodists, had been made obsolete by the growth of rationalism. Still the new public wanted something more savoury than its elegant teachers had given; and, if sermons had ceased to be so stimulating as of old, it could find it in secular moralisers. Defoe, always keenly alive to the general taste, had tried to supply the demand not only by his queer *History of the Devil* but by appending a set of moral reflections to *Robinson Crusoe* and other edifying works, which disgusted Charles Lamb by their petty tradesman morality, and which hardly represent a very lofty ideal. But the recognised representative of the moralists was the ponderous Samuel Johnson. It is hard when reading the *Rambler* to recognise the massive common sense and deep feeling struggling with the ponderous verbiage and elephantine facetiousness ; yet it was not only a treasure of wisdom to the learned ladies, Mrs. Chapone, and Mrs. Elizabeth Carter and the like, who were now beginning to appear, but was received, without provoking ridicule, by the whole literary class. *Rasselas*, in spite of its formality, is still a very impressive book. The literary critic may amuse himself with the question how Johnson came to acquire the peculiar style which imposed upon contemporaries and excited the ridicule of the next generation. According to Boswell, it was due to his reading of Sir Thomas Browne, and a kind of reversion to the earlier period in which the Latinisms of Browne were still natural, when the revolt to simple prose had not begun. Addison, at any rate, as Boswell truly remarks, writes like a 'companion,' and Johnson like a teacher. He puts on his academical robes to deliver his message to mankind, and is no longer the Wit, echoing the coffee-house talk, but the moralist, who looks indeed at actual life, but stands well apart and knows many hours of melancholy and hypochondria. He preaches the morality of his time—the morality of Richardson and Young—only tempered by a hearty contempt for cant, sentimentalism, and all unreality, and expressing his deeper and stronger nature. The style, however acquired, has the idiosyncrasy of the man himself; but I shall have to speak of the Johnsonian view in the next period, when he became the acknowledged literary dictator and expressed one main tendency of the period.

Meanwhile Richardson, as Johnson put it, had been teaching the passions to move at the command of virtue. In other words, Richardson had discovered an incomparably more effective way of preaching a popular sermon. He had begun, as we know, by writing a series of edifying letters to young women; and expounded the same method in *Pamela*, and afterwards in the famous *Clarissa Harlowe* and *Sir Charles Grandison*. All his books are deliberate attempts to embody his ideal in model representatives of the society of his day. He might have taken a suggestion from Bunyan; who besides his great religious allegory and the curious life of *Mr. Badman*, couched a moral lesson in a description of the actual tradesman of his time. Allegory was now to be supplanted by fiction. The man was to take the place of the personified virtue and vice. Defoe had already shown the power of downright realistic story-telling; and Richardson perhaps learnt something from him when he was drawing his minute and vivid portraits of the people who might at any rate pass for being realities. I must take for granted that Richardson was a man of genius, without adding a word as to its precise quality. I need only repeat one familiar remark. Richardson was a typical tradesman of the period; he was the industrious apprentice who marries his master's daughter; he lived between Hammersmith and Salisbury Court as a thorough middle-class cockney, and had not an idea beyond those common to his class; he accepted the ordinary creeds and conventions; he looked upon free-thinkers with such horror that he will not allow even his worst villains to be religious sceptics; he shares the profound reverence of the shopkeepers for the upper classes who are his customers, and he rewards virtue with a coach and six. And yet this mild little man, with the very narrowest intellectual limitations, writes a book which makes a mark not only in England but in Europe, and is imitated by Rousseau in the book which set more than one generation weeping; *Clarissa Harlowe*, moreover, was accepted as the masterpiece of its kind, and she moved not only Englishmen but Germans and Frenchmen to sympathetic tears. One explanation is that Richardson is regarded as the inventor of 'sentimentalism.' The word, as one of his correspondents tells him, was a novelty about 1749, and was then supposed to include anything that was clever and agreeable. I do not myself believe that anybody invented the mode of feeling; but it is true that Richardson was the first writer who definitely turned it to account for a new literary genus. Sentimentalism, I suppose, means, roughly speaking, indulgence in emotion for its own sake. The sentimentalist does not weep because painful thoughts are forced upon him but because he finds weeping pleasant in itself. He appreciates the 'luxury of grief.' (The phrase is used in Brown's *Barbarossa*; I don't know who invented it.) Certainly the discovery was not new. The charms of melancholy had been recognised by Jaques in the forest of Arden and sung by various later poets; but sentimentalism at the earlier period naturally took the form of religious meditation upon death and judgment. Young and Hervey are religious sentimentalists, who have also an eye to literary elegance. Wesley was far too masculine and sensible to be a sentimentalist; his emotions impel him to vigorous action; and are much too serious to be cultivated for their own sakes or to be treated æsthetically. But the general sense that something is not in order in the general state of things, without as yet any definite aim for the vague discontent, was shared by the true sentimentalist. Richardson's sentimentalism is partly unconscious. He is a moralist very much in earnest, preaching a very practical and not very exalted morality. It is his moral purpose, his insistence upon the edifying point of view, his singular fertility in finding illustrations for his doctrines, which makes him a sentimentalist. I will confess that the last time I read *Clarissa Harlowe* it affected me with a kind of disgust. We wonder sometimes at the coarse nerves of our ancestors, who could see on the stage any quantity of murders and ghosts and miscellaneous horrors. Richardson gave me the same shock from the elaborate detail in which he tells the story of

Clarissa; rubbing our noses, if I may say so, in all her agony, and squeezing the last drop of bitterness out of every incident. I should have liked some symptom that he was anxious to turn his eyes from the tragedy instead of giving it so minutely as to suggest that he enjoys the spectacle. Books sometimes owe part of their success, as I fear we must admit, to the very fact that they are in bad taste. They attract the contemporary audience by exaggerating and over-weighting the new vein of sentiment which they have discovered. That, in fact, seems to be the reason why in spite of all authority, modern readers find it difficult to read Richardson through. We know, at any rate, how it affected one great contemporary. This incessant strain upon the moral in question (a very questionable moral it is) struck Fielding as mawkish and unmanly. Richardson seemed to be a narrow, straitlaced preacher, who could look at human nature only from the conventional point of view, and thought that because he was virtuous there should be no more cakes and ale.

Fielding's revolt produced his great novels, and the definite creation of an entirely new form of art which was destined to a long and vigorous life. He claimed to be the founder of a new province in literature, and saw with perfect clearness what was to be its nature. The old romances which had charmed the seventeenth century were still read occasionally: Lady Mary Wortley Montagu, for example, and Dr. Johnson had enjoyed them, and Chesterfield, at a later period, has to point out to his son that Calprenède's *Cassandra* has become ridiculous. The short story, of which Mrs. Behn was the last English writer, was more or less replaced by the little sketches in the *Spectator*; and Defoe had shown the attractiveness of a downright realistic narrative of a series of adventures. But whatever precedents may be found, our unfortunate ancestors had not yet the true modern novel. Fielding had, like other hack authors, written for the stage and tried to carry on the Congreve tradition. But the stage had declined. The best products, perhaps, were the *Beggar's Opera* and *Chrononhotonthologos* and Fielding's own *Tom Thumb*. When Fielding tried to make use of the taste for political lampoons, the result was the Act of Parliament which in 1737 introduced the licensing system. The Shakespearian drama, it is true, was coming into popularity with the help of Fielding's great friend, Garrick; but no new Shakespeare appeared to write modern *Hamlets* and *Othellos*; Johnson tried to supply his place with the ponderous *Irene*, and John Home followed with *Douglas* of 'My name is Norval' fame. The tragedies were becoming more dreary. Characteristic of Fielding was his admiration of Lillo, whose *George Barnwell* (1730) and *Fatal Curiosity* (about 1736), the last of them brought out under Fielding's own management, were remarkable attempts to revive tragedies by going to real life. It is plain, however, that the theatre is no longer the appropriate organ of the reading classes. The licensing act seems to have expressed the general feeling which, if we call it Puritan, must be Puritan in a sense which described the general middle-class prejudices. The problem which Fielding had to solve was to find a literary form which should meet the tastes of the new public, who could not be drawn to the theatre, and which yet should have some of the characteristics which had hitherto been confined to the dramatic form. That was the problem which was triumphantly solved by *Tom Jones*. The story is no longer a mere series of adventures, such as that which happened to Crusoe or Gil Blas, connected by the fact that they happen to the same person; nor a prolonged religious or moral tract, showing how evil will be punished and virtue rewarded. It implies a dramatic situation which can be developed without being hampered by the necessities of stage-representation; and which can give full scope to a realistic portrait of nature as it is under all the familiar circumstances of time and place. This novel, which fulfilled those conditions, has ever since continued to flourish; although a long time was to elapse before any one could approach the merits of the first inventor. In all ages, I suppose, the great artist, whether dramatist or epic poet or novelist, has more or less consciously had the aim which Fielding implicitly claims for himself; that is, to portray human nature. Every great artist, again, must, in one sense, be thoroughly 'realistic.' The word has acquired an irrelevant connotation: but I mean that his vision of the world must correspond to the genuine living convictions of his time. He only ceases to be a realist in that wide sense of the word when he deliberately affects beliefs which have lost their vitality and uses the old mythology, for example, as convenient machinery, when it has ceased to have any real hold upon the minds of their contemporaries. So far Defoe and Richardson and Fielding were perfectly right and deservedly successful because they described the actual human beings whom they saw before them, instead of regarding a setting forth of plain facts as something below the dignity of the artist. Every new departure in literature thrives in proportion as it abandons the old conventions which have become mere survivals. Each of them, in his way, felt the need of appealing to the new class of readers by direct portraiture of the readers themselves. Fielding's merit is his thorough appreciation of this necessity. He will give you men as he sees them, with perfect impartiality and photographic accuracy. His hearty appreciation of genuine work is characteristic. He admires Lillo, as I have said, for giving George Barnwell instead of the conventional stage hero; and his friend Hogarth, who was in pictorial art what he was in fiction, and paints the 'Rake's Progress' without bothering about old masters or the grand style; and he is enthusiastic about Garrick because he makes Hamlet's fear of the ghost so natural that Partridge takes it for a mere matter of course. Downright, forcible appeals to fact—contempt for the artificial and conventional—are his strength, though they also imply his weakness. Fielding, in fact, is the ideal John Bull; the 'good buffalo,' as Taine calls him, the big, full-blooded, vigorous mass of roast-beef who will stand no nonsense, and whose contempt for the fanciful and arbitrary tends towards the coarse and materialistic. That corresponds to the contrast between Richardson and Fielding; and may help to explain why the sentimentalism which Fielding despised yet corresponded to a vague feeling after a real element of interest. But, in truth, our criticism, I think, applies as much to Richardson as to Fielding. Realism, taken in what I should call the right sense, is not properly opposed to 'idealism'; it points to one of the two poles towards which all literary art should be directed. The artist is a realist so far as he deals with the actual life and the genuine beliefs of his time; but he is an idealist so far as he sees the most essential facts and utters the deepest and most permanent truths in his own dialect. His work should be true to life and give the essence of actual human nature, and also express emotions and thoughts common to the men of all times. Now that is the weak side of the fiction of this period. We may read *Clarissa Harlowe* and *Tom Jones* with unstinted admiration; but we feel that we are in a confined atmosphere. There are regions of thought and feeling which seem to lie altogether beyond their province. Fielding, in his way, was a bit of a philosopher, though he is too much convinced that Locke and Hoadley have said the last words in theology and philosophy. Parson Adams is a most charming person in his way, but his intellectual outlook is decidedly limited. That may not trouble us much; but we have also the general feeling that we are living in a little provincial society which somehow takes its own special arrangements to be part of the eternal order of nature. The worthy Richardson is aware that there are a great many rakes and infamous persons about; but it never occurs to him that there can be any speculation outside the Thirty-nine Articles; and though Fielding perceives a great many abuses in the actual administration of the laws and the political system, he regards the social order, with its squires and parsons and attorneys as the only conceivable state of things. In other words they, and I might add their successor Smollett, represent all the prejudices and narrow assumptions of the quiet, respectable, and in many ways worthy and domestically excellent, middle-class of the day; which, on the whole, is determined not to look too deeply into awkward questions, but to go along sturdily working out its own conceptions and plodding along on well-established lines.

Another literary movement is beginning which is to lead to the sense of this deficiency. The nobleman, growing rich and less absorbed in the political world, has time and leisure to cultivate his tastes, becomes, as I have said, a dilettante, and sends his son to make the grand tour as a regular part of his education. Some demon whispers to him, as Pope puts it, Visto, have a taste! He buys books and pictures, takes to architecture and landscape-gardening, and becomes a 'collector.' The instinct of 'collecting' is, I suppose, natural, and its development is connected with some curious results. One of the favourite objects of ridicule of the past essayists was the virtuoso. There was something to them inexpressibly absurd in a passion for buying odds and ends. Pope, Arbuthnot, and Gay made a special butt of Dr. Woodward, possessor of a famous ancient shield and other antiquities. Equally absurd, they thought, was his passion for fossils. He made one of the first collections of such objects, saw that they really had a scientific interest, and founded at Cambridge the first professorship of geology. Another remarkable collector was Sir Hans Sloane, who had brought home a great number of plants from Jamaica and founded the botanic garden at Chelsea. His servant, James Salter, set up the famous Don Saltero's museum in the same place, containing, as Steele tell us, '10,000 gimcracks, including a "petrified crab" from China and Pontius Pilate's wife's chambermaid's sister's hat.' Don Saltero and his master seemed equally ridiculous; and Young in his satires calls Sloane 'the foremost toyman of his time,' and describes him as adoring a pin of Queen Elizabeth's. Sloane's collections were bought for the nation and became the foundation of the British Museum; when (1753) Horace Walpole remarks that they might be worth £80,000 for anybody who loved hippopotamuses, sharks with one ear, and spiders as big as geese. Scientific research, that is, revealed itself to contemporaries as a childish and absurd monomania, unworthy of a man of sense. John Hunter had not yet begun to form the unequalled museum of physiology, and even the scientific collectors could have but a dim perception of the importance of a minute observation of natural phenomena. The contempt for such collections naturally accompanied a contempt for the antiquary, another variety of the same species. The study of old documents and ancient buildings seemed to be a simple eccentricity. Thomas Hearne, the Oxford antiquary, was a typical case. He devoted himself to the study of old records and published a series of English Chronicles which were of essential service to English historians. To his contemporaries this study seemed to be as worthless as Woodward's study of fossils. Like other monomaniacs he became crusty and sour for want of sympathy. His like-minded contemporary, Carte, ruined the prospects of his history by letting out his belief in the royal power of curing by touch. Antiquarianism, though providing invaluable material for history, seemed to be a silly crotchet, and to imply a hatred to sound Whiggism and modern enlightenment, so long as the Wit and the intelligent person of quality looked upon the past simply as the period of Gothic barbarism. But an approximation is beginning to take place. The relation is indicated by the case of Horace Walpole, a man whose great abilities have been concealed by his obvious affectations. Two of Walpole's schoolfellows at Eton were Gray and William Cole. Cole, the Cambridge antiquary, who tried to do for his own university what Woodward had done for Oxford, was all but a Catholic, and in political sympathies agreed with Hearne and Carte. Walpole was a thorough Whig and a freethinker, so long, at least, as freethinking did not threaten danger to comfortable sinecures bestowed upon the sons of Whig ministers. But Cole became Walpole's antiquarian oracle. When Walpole came back from the grand tour, with nothing particular to do except spend his income, he found one amusement in dabbling in antiquarian research. He discovered, among other things, that even a Gothic cathedral could be picturesque, and in 1750 set about building a 'little Gothic Castle' at Strawberry Hill. The Gothic was of course the most superficial imitation; but it became the first of a long line of similar imitations growing gradually more elaborate with results of which we all have our own opinion. To Walpole himself Strawberry Hill was a mere plaything, and he would not have wished to be taken too seriously; as his romance of the *Castle of Otranto* was a literary squib at which he laughed himself, though it became the forefather of a great literary school. The process may be regarded as logical: the previous generation, rejoicing in its own enlightenment, began to recognise the difference between present and past more clearly than its ancestors had done; but generally inferred that the men of old had been barbarians. The Tory and Jacobite who clings to the past praises its remains with blind affection, and can see nothing in the present but corruption and destruction of the foundations of society. The indifferent dilettante, caring little for any principles and mainly desirous of amusement, discovers a certain charm in the old institutions while he professes to despise them in theory. That means one of the elements of the complex sentiment which we describe as romanticism. The past is obsolete, but it is pretty enough to be used in making new playthings. The reconciliation will be reached when the growth of historical inquiry leads men to feel that past and present are parts of a continuous series, and to look upon their ancestors neither as simply ridiculous nor as objects of blind admiration. The historical sense was, in fact, growing: and Walpole's other friend,

Gray, may represent the literary version. The Queen Anne school, though it despised the older literature, had still a certain sneaking regard for it. Addison, for example, pays some grudging compliments to Chaucer and Spenser, though he is careful to point out the barbarism of their taste. Pope, like all poets, had loved Spenser in his boyhood and was well read in English poetry. It was mighty simple of Rowe, he said, to try to write in the style of Shakespeare, that is, in the style of a bad age. Yet he became one of the earliest, and far from one of the worst, editors of Shakespeare; and the growth of literary interest in Shakespeare is one of the characteristic symptoms of the period. Pope had contemplated a history of English poetry which was taken up by Gray and finally executed by Warton. The development of an interest in literary history naturally led to new departures. The poets of the period, Gray and Collins and the Wartons, are no longer members of the little circle with strict codes of taste. They are scholars and students not shut up within the metropolitan area. There has been a controversy as to whether Gray's unproductiveness is partly to be ascribed to his confinement to a narrow and, it seems, to a specially stupid academical circle at Cambridge. Anyway, living apart from the world of politicians and fine gentlemen, he had the opportunity to become the most learned of English poets and to be at home in a wide range of literature representing a great variety of models. As the antiquary begins to rise to the historian, the poetical merits recognised in the less regular canons become manifest. Thomson, trying to write a half-serious imitation of Spenser, made his greatest success by a kind of accident in the *Castle of Indolence* (1748); Thomas Warton's Observation on the *Faery Queene* in 1757 was an illustration of the influence of historical criticism. I need not say how Collins was interested by Highland superstition and Gray impressed by Mallet's *Northern Antiquities*, and how in other directions the labours of the antiquarian were beginning to provide materials for the poetical imagination. Gray and Collins still held to the main Pope principles. They try to be clear and simple and polished, and their trick of personifying abstract qualities indicates the philosophical doctrine which was still acceptable. The special principle, however, which they were beginning to recognise is that indicated by Joseph Warton's declaration in his *Essay on Pope* (1757).

'The fashion of moralising in verse,' he said, had been pushed too far, and he proceeded to startle the orthodox by placing Spenser above Pope. The heresy gave so much offence, it is said, that he did not venture to bring out his second volume for twenty-five years. The point made by Warton marks, in fact, the critical change. The weak side of the Pope school had been the subordination of the imagination to the logical theory. Poetry tends to become rhymed prose because the poet like the preacher has to expound doctrines and to prove by argument. He despises the old mythology and the romantic symbolism because the theory was obviously absurd to a man of the world, and to common sense. He believes that Homer was deliberately conveying an allegory: and an allegory, whether of Homer or of Spenser, is a roundabout and foolish way of expressing the truth. A philosopher—and a poem is versified philosophy—should express himself as simply and directly as possible. But, as soon as you begin to appreciate the charm of ancient poetry, to be impressed by Scandinavian Sagas or Highland superstition or Welsh bards, or allow yourself to enjoy Spenser's idealised knights and ladies in spite of their total want of common sense, or to appreciate *Paradise Lost* although you no longer accept Milton's scheme of theology, it becomes plain that the specially poetic charm must consist in something else; that it can appeal to the emotions and the imagination, though the doctrine which it embodies is as far as possible from convincing your reason. The discovery has a bearing upon what is called the love of Nature. Even Thomson and his followers still take the didactic view of Nature. They are half ashamed of their interest in mere dead objects, but can treat skies and mountains as a text for discourses upon Natural Theology. But Collins and Gray and Warton are beginning to perceive that the pleasure which we receive from a beautiful prospect, whether of a mountain or of an old abbey, is something which justifies itself and may be expressed in poetry without tagging a special moral to its tail. Yet the sturdy common sense represented by Fielding and Johnson is slow to accept this view, and the romantic view of things has still for him a touch of sentimentalism and affectation, and indicates the dilettante rather than the serious thinker, and Pope still represents the orthodox creed though symptoms of revolt are slowly showing themselves.

V

(1763-1788)

I NOW come to the generation which preceded the outbreak of the French Revolution. Social and political movements are beginning to show themselves in something of their modern form, and suggest most interesting problems for the speculative historian. At the same time, if we confine ourselves to the purely literary region, it is on the whole a period of stagnation. Johnson is the acknowledged dictator, and Johnson, the 'last of the Tories,' upholds the artistic canons of Dryden and Pope, though no successor arises to produce new works at all comparable with theirs. The school, still ostensibly dominant, has lost its power of stimulating genius; and as yet no new school has arisen to take its place. Wordsworth and Coleridge and Scott were still at college, and Byron in the nursery, at the end of the period. There is a kind of literary interregnum, though not a corresponding stagnation of speculative and political energy.

Looking, in the first place, at the active world, the great fact of the time is the series of changes to which we give the name of the industrial revolution. The growth of commercial and manufacturing enterprise which had been going on quietly and continuously had been suddenly accelerated. Glasgow and Liverpool and Manchester and Birmingham were becoming great towns, and the factory system was being developed, profoundly modifying the old relation of the industrial classes. England was beginning to aim at commercial supremacy, and politics were to be more than ever dominated by the interests of the 'moneyed man,' or, as we now call them, 'capitalists.' Essentially connected with these changes is another characteristic development. Social problems were arising. The growth of the manufactory system and the accumulation of masses of town population, for example, forced attention to the problem of pauperism, and many attempts of various kinds were being made to deal with it. The same circumstances were beginning to rouse an interest in education; it had suddenly struck people that on Sundays, at least, children might be taught their letters so far as to enable them to spell out their Bible. The inadequacy of the police and prison systems to meet the new requirements roused the zeal of many, and led to some reforms. As the British Empire extended we began to become sensible of certain correlative duties; the impeachment of Warren Hastings showed that we had scruples about treating India simply as a place where 'nabobs' are to accumulate fortunes; and the slave-trade suggested questions of conscience which at the end of the period were to prelude an agitation in some ways unprecedented.

In the political world again we have the first appearance of a distinctly democratic movement. The struggle over Wilkes during the earlier years began a contest which was to last through generations. The American War of Independence emphasised party issues, and in some sense heralded the French Revolution. I only note one point. The British 'Whig' of those days represented two impulses which gradually diverged. There was the home-bred Whiggism of Wilkes and Horne Tooke—the Whiggism of which the stronghold was in the city of London, with such heroes as Lord Mayor Beckford, whose statue in the Guildhall displays him hurling defiance at poor George III. This party embodies the dissatisfaction of the man of business with the old system which cramped his energies. In the name of liberty he demands 'self-government'; not greater vigour in the Executive but less interference and a freer hand for the capitalist. He believes in individual enterprise. He accepts the good old English principle that the man who pays taxes should have a voice in spending them; but he appeals not to an abstract political principle but to tradition. The reformer, as so often happens, calls himself a restorer; his political bible begins with the great charter and comes down to the settlement of 1688. Meanwhile the true revolutionary movement — represented by Paine and Godwin, appeals to the doctrines of natural equality and the rights of man. It is unequivocally democratic, and implies a growing cleavage between the working man and the capitalists. It repudiates all tradition, and aspires to recast the whole social order. Instead of proposing simply to diminish the influence of government, it really tends to centralisation and the transference of power to the lower classes. This genuine revolutionary principle did not become conspicuous in England until it was introduced by the contagion from France, and even then it remained an exotic. For the present the Whig included all who opposed the Toryism of George III. The difference between the Whig and the Radical was still latent, though to be manifested in the near future. When the 'new Whigs,' as Burke called them, Fox and Sheridan, welcomed the French Revolution in 1789, they saw in it a constitutional movement of the English type and not a thorough-going democratic movement which would level all classes, and transfer the political supremacy to a different social stratum.

This implies a dominant characteristic of the English political movement. It was led, to use a later phrase, by Whigs not Radicals; by men who fully accepted the British constitution, and proposed to remove abuses, not to recast the whole system. The Whig wished to carry out more thoroughly the platform accepted in 1688, to replace decaying by sound timbers; but not to reconstruct from the base or to override tradition by abstract and obsolete theories. His desire for change was limited by a strong though implicit conservatism. This characteristic is reflected in the sphere of speculative activity. Philosophy was represented by the Scottish school whose watchword was common sense. Reid opposed the scepticism of Hume which would lead, as he held, to knocking his head against a post—a course clearly condemned by common sense; but instead of soaring into transcendental and ontological regions, he stuck to 'Baconian induction' and a psychology founded upon experience. Hume himself, as I have said, had written for the speculative few not for the vulgar; and he had now turned from the chase of metaphysical refinements to historical inquiry. Interest in history had become characteristic of the time. The growth of a stable, complex, and continuous social order implies the formation of a corporate memory. Masses of records had already been accumulated by antiquaries who had constructed rather annals than history, in which the series of events was given without much effort to arrange them in literary form or trace the causal connection. In France, however, Montesquieu had definitely established the importance of applying the historical method to political problems; and Voltaire had published some of his brilliant surveys which attempt to deal with the social characteristics as well as the mere records of battles and conquests. Hume's *History*, admirably written, gave Englishmen the first opportunity of enjoying a lucid survey of the conspicuous facts previously embedded in ponderous antiquarian phrases. Hume was one of the triumvirate who produced the recognised masterpieces of contemporary literature. Robertson's theories are, I take it, superseded: but his books, especially the *Charles V.*, not only gave broad surveys but suggested generalisations as to the development of institutions, which, like most generalisations, were mainly wrong, but stimulated further inquiry. Gibbon, the third of the triumvirate, uniting the power of presenting great panoramas of history with thorough scholarship and laborious research, produced the great work which has not been, if it ever can be, superseded. A growing interest in history thus led to some of the chief writings of the time, as we can see that it was the natural outgrowth of the intellectual position. The rapid widening of the historical horizon made even a bare survey useful, and led to some recognition of the importance of guiding and correcting political and social theory by careful investigation of past experience. The historian began to feel an ambition to deal in philosophical theories. He was, moreover, touched by the great scientific movement. A complete survey of the intellectual history of the time would of course have to deal with the great men who were laying the foundations of the modern physical sciences; such as Black, and Priestley, and Cavendish, and Hunter. It would indeed, have to point out how small was the total amount of such knowledge in comparison with the vast superstructure which has been erected in the last century. The foundation of the Royal Institution at the end of the eighteenth century marks, perhaps, the point at which the importance of physical science began to impress the popular imagination. But great thinkers had long recognised the necessity of applying scientific method in the sphere of social and political investigation. Two men especially illustrate the tendency and the particular turn which it took in England. Adam Smith's great book in 1776 applied scientific method to political economy. Smith is distinguished from his French predecessors by the historical element of his work; by his careful study, that is, of economic history, and his consequent presentation of his theory not as a body of absolute and quasi-mathematical truth, but as resting upon the experience and applicable to the concrete facts of his time. His limitation is equally characteristic. He investigated the play of the industrial mechanism with too little reference to the thorough interdependence of economic and other social conditions. Showing how that mechanism adapts itself to supply and demand, he comes to hold that the one thing necessary is to leave free play to competition, and that the one essential force is the individual's desire for his own material interests. He became, therefore, the prophet of letting things alone. That doctrine—whatever its merits or defects—implies acquiescence in the existing order, and is radically opposed to a demand for a reconstruction of society. This is most clearly illustrated by the other thinker Jeremy Bentham. Bentham, unlike Smith, shared the contempt for history of the absolute theorists, and was laying down a theory conceived in the spirit of absolutism which became the creed of the uncompromising political radicals of the next generation. But it is characteristic that Bentham was not, during the eighteenth century, a Radical at all. He altogether repudiated and vigorously denounced the 'Rights of Men' doctrines of Rousseau and his followers, and regarded the Declaration of Independence in which they were embodied as a mere hotchpotch of absurdity. He is determined to be thoroughly empirical—to take men as he found them. But his utilitarianism supposed that men's views of happiness and utility were uniform and clear, and that all that was wanted was to show them the means by which their ends could be reached. Then, he thought, rulers and subjects would be equally ready to apply his principles. He fully accepted Adam Smith's theory of non-interference in economical matters; and his view of philosophy in the lump was that there was no such thing, only a heap of obsolete fallacies and superstitions which would be easily dispersed by the application of a little downright common sense. Bentham's utilitarianism, again, is congenial to the whole intellectual movement. His ethical theory was substantially identical with that of Paley—the most conspicuous writer upon theology of the generation,—and Paley is as thoroughly empirical in his theology as in his ethics, and makes the truth of religion essentially a question of historical and scientific evidence.

It follows that neither in practice nor in speculative questions were the English thinkers of the time prescient of any coming revolution. They denounced abuses, but they had regarded abuses as removable excrescences on a satisfactory system. They were content to appeal to common sense, and to leave philosophers to wrangle over ultimate results. They might be, and in fact were, stirring questions which would lead to far more vital disputes ; but for the present they were unconscious of the future, and content to keep the old machinery going though desiring to improve its efficiency. The characteristic might be elucidated by comparison with the other great European literatures. In France, Voltaire had begun about 1762 his crusade against orthodoxy, or, as he calls it, his attempt to crush the infamous. He was supported by his allies, the Encyclopædists. While Helvétius and Holbach were expounding materialism and atheism, Rousseau had enunciated the political doctrines which were to be applied to the Revolution, and elsewhere had uttered that sentimental deism which was to be so dear to many of his readers. Our neighbours, in short, after their characteristic fashion, were pushing logic to its consequences, and fully awake to the approach of an impending catastrophe. In Germany the movement took the philosophical and literary shape. Lessing's critical writings had heralded the change. Goethe, after giving utterance to passing phases of thought, was rising to become the embodiment of a new ideal of intellectual culture. Schiller passed through the storm and stress period and developed into the greatest national dramatist. Kant had awakened from his dogmatic theory, and the publication of the *Critique of Pure Reason* in 1781 had awakened the philosophical world of Germany. In both countries the study of earlier English literature, of the English deists and freethinkers, of Shakespeare and of Richardson, had had great influence, and had been the occasion of new developments. But it seemed as though England had ceased to be the originator of ideas, and was for the immediate future at least to receive political and philosophical impulses from France and Germany. To explain the course taken in the different societies, to ask how far it might be due to difference of characteristics, and of political constitutions, of social organism and individual genius, would be a very pretty but rather large problem. I refer to it simply to illustrate the facts, to emphasise the quiet, orderly, if you will, sleepy movement of English thought which, though combined with great practical energy and vigorous investigation of the neighbouring departments of inquiry, admitted of comparative indifference to the deeper issues involved. It did not generate that stimulus to literary activity due to the dawning of new ideas and the opening of wide vistas of speculation. When the French Revolution broke out, it took Englishmen, one may say, by surprise, and except by a few keen observers or rare disciples of Rousseau, was as unexpected as the earthquake of Lisbon.

Let us glance, now, at the class which was to carry on the literary tradition. It is known to us best through Boswell, and its characteristics are represented by Johnson's favourite club. In one of his talks with Boswell the great man amused himself by showing how the club might form itself into a university. Every branch of knowledge and thought might, he thought, be represented, though it must be admitted that some of the professors suggested were scarcely up to the mark. The social variety is equally remarkable. Among the thirty or forty members elected before Johnson's death, there were the lights of literature ; Johnson himself and Goldsmith,

Adam Smith and Gibbon, and others of less fame. The aristocratic element was represented by Beauclerk and by half a dozen peers, such as the amiable Lord Charlemont; Burke, Fox, Sheridan, and Wyndham represent political as well as literary eminence; three or four bishops represent Church authority; legal luminaries included Dunning, William Scott (the famous Lord Stowell), Sir Robert Chambers, and the amazingly versatile Sir William Jones. Boswell and Langton are also cultivated country gentlemen; Sir Joseph Banks stood for science, and three other names show the growing respect for art. The amiable Dr. Burney was a musician who had raised the standard of his calling; Garrick had still more conspicuously gained social respect for the profession of actor; and Sir Joshua Reynolds was the representative of the English school of painters, whose works still impress upon us the beauty of our great-grandmothers and the charm of their children, and suggest the existence of a really dignified and pure domestic life in a class too often remembered by the reckless gambling and loose morality of the gilded youth of the day. To complete the picture of the world in which Johnson was at home we should have to add from the outer sphere such types as Thrale, the prosperous brewer, and the lively Mrs. Thrale and Mrs. Montague, who kept a salon and was president of the 'Blues.' The feminine society which was beginning to write our novels was represented by Miss Burney and Hannah More; and the thriving booksellers who were beginning to become publishers, such as Strahan and the Dillys, at whose house he had the famous meeting with the reprobate Wilkes. To many of us, I suppose, an intimacy with that Johnsonian group has been a first introduction to an interest in English literature. Thanks to Boswell, we can hear its talk more distinctly than that of any later circle. When we compare it to the society of an earlier time, one or two points are conspicuous. Johnson's club was to some extent a continuation of the clubs of Queen Anne's time. But the Wits of the earlier period who met at taverns to drink with the patrons were a much smaller and more dependent body. What had since happened had been the growth of a great comfortable middle-class—meaning by middle-class the upper stratum, the professional men, the lawyers, clergymen, physicians, the merchants who had been enriched by the growth of commerce and manufactures; the country gentlemen whose rents had risen, and who could come to London and rub off their old rusticity. The aristocracy is still in possession of great wealth and political power, but beneath it has grown up an independent society which is already beginning to be the most important social stratum and the chief factor in political and social development. It has sufficient literary cultivation to admit the distinguished authors and artists who are becoming independent enough to take their place in its ranks and appear at its tables and rule the conversation. The society is still small enough to have in the club a single representative body and one man for dictator. Johnson succeeded in this capacity to Pope, Dryden, and his namesake Ben, but he was the last of the race. Men like Carlyle and Macaulay, who had a similar distinction in later days, could only be leaders of a single group or section in the more complex society of their time, though it was not yet so multitudinous and chaotic as the literary class has become in our own. Talk could still be good, because the comparatively small society was constantly meeting, and each prepared to take his part in the game, and was not being swept away distractedly into a miscellaneous vortex of all sorts and conditions of humanity. Another fact is conspicuous. The environment, we may say, of the man of letters was congenial. He shared and uttered the opinions of the class to which he belonged. Buckle gives a striking account of the persecution to which the French men of letters were exposed at this period; Voltaire, Buffon, and Rousseau, Diderot, Marmontel, and Morellet, besides a whole series of inferior authors, had their books suppressed and were themselves either exiled or imprisoned. There was a state of war in which almost the whole literary class attacked the established creed while the rulers replied by force instead of argument. In England men of letters were allowed, with a few exceptions, to say what they thought, and simply shared the average beliefs of their class and their rulers. If some leant towards freethinking, the general tendency of the Johnson circle was harshly opposed to any revolutionary movement, and authors were satisfied with the creeds as with the institutions amid which they lived.

The English literary class was thus content to utter the beliefs prevalent in the social stratum to which the chief writers belonged—a stratum which had no special grievances and no revolutionary impulses, and which could make its voice sufficiently heard though by methods which led to no explicit change in the constitution, and suggests only a change in the forces which really lay behind them. The chief political changes mean for the present that 'public opinion' was acquiring more power; that the newspaper press as its organ was especially growing in strength; that Parliament was thrown open to the reporter, and speeches addressed to the constituencies as well as to the Houses of Parliament, and therefore the authority of the legislation becoming more amenable to the opinions of the constituency. That is to say, again, that the journalist and orator were growing in power and a corresponding direction given to literary talent. The Wilkes agitation led to the *Letters of Junius*—one of the most conspicuous models of the style of the period; and some of the newspapers which were to live through the next century began to appear in the following years. This period again might almost be called the culminating period of English rhetoric. The speeches of Pitt and Burke and Fox and Sheridan in the House of Commons and at the impeachment of Warren Hastings must be regarded from the literary as well as the political point of view, though in most cases the decay of the temporary interests involved has been fatal to their permanence. The speeches are still real speeches, intended to affect the audience addressed, and yet partly intended also for the reporters. When the audience becomes merely the pretext, and the real aim is to address the public, the speech tends to become a pamphlet in disguise and loses its rhetorical character. I may remark in passing that almost the only legal speeches which, so far as my knowledge goes, are still readable, were those of Erskine, who, after trying the careers of a sailor and a soldier, found the true application for his powers in oratory. Though his legal knowledge is said to have been slight, the conditions of the time enabled him in addressing a British jury to put forward a political manifesto and to display singular literary skill. Burke, however, is the typical figure. Had he been a German he might have been a Lessing, and the author of the *Sublime and Beautiful* might, like the author of *Laokoon*, have stimulated his countrymen by literary criticism. Or he might have obtained a professorship or a court preacher-ship and, like Herder, have elaborated ideas towards the future of a philosophy of history. In England he was drawn into the political vortex, and in that capacity delivered speeches which also appeared as pamphlets, and which must rank among the great masterpieces of English literature. I need not inquire whether he lost more by giving to party what was meant for mankind, or whether his philosophy did not gain more by the necessity of constant application to the actual facts of the time. That necessity no doubt limited both the amount and the systematic completeness of his writings, though it also emphasised some of their highest merits. The English political order tended in any case to divert a great deal of literary ability into purely political channels—a peculiarity which it has not yet lost. Burke is the typical instance of this combination, and illustrates most forcibly the point to which I have already adverted. Johnson, as we know, was a mass of obstinate Tory prejudice, and held that the devil was the first Whig. He held at bottom, I think, that politics touched only the surface of human life; that 'kings or laws,' as he put it, can cause or cure only a small part of the evils which we suffer, and that some authority is absolutely necessary, and that it matters little whether it be the authority of a French monarch or an English parliament. The Whig he thought objected to authority on principle, and was therefore simply subversive. Something of the same opinion was held by Johnson's circle in general. They were conservative both in politics and theology, and English politics and theological disputes did not obviously raise the deeper issues. Even the devil-descended Whig—especially the variety represented by Burke—was as far as possible from representing what he took for the diabolic agency. Burke represents above all things the political application of the historical spirit of the period. His hatred for metaphysics, for discussions of abstract rights instead of practical expediency; his exaltation of 'prescription' and 'tradition'; his admiration for Montesquieu and his abhorrence of Rousseau; his idolatry of the British constitution, and in short his whole political doctrine from first to last, implies the profound conviction of the truth of the principles embodied in a thorough historical method. Nobody, I think, was ever more consistent in his first principles, though his horror of the Revolution no doubt led him so to exaggerate one side of his teaching that he was led to denounce some of the consequences which naturally followed from other aspects of his doctrine. The schism between the old and the new Whigs was not to be foreseen during this period, nor the coming into the foreground of the deeper problems involved.

I may now come to the purely literary movement. I have tried to show that neither in philosophy, theology, nor political and social strata, was there any belief in the necessity of radical changes, or prescience of a coming alteration of the intellectual atmosphere. Speculation, like politics, could advance quietly along the old paths without fearing that they might lead to a precipice ; and society, in spite of very vigorous and active controversy upon the questions which decided it was in the main self-satisfied, complacent, and comfortable. Adherence to the old system is after all the general rule, and it is of the change not the persistence that we require some account. At the beginning of our period, Pope's authority was still generally admitted, although many symptoms of discontent had appeared, and Warton was proposing to lower him from the first to the second rank. The two most brilliant writers who achieved fame in the early years of George III., Goldsmith and Sterne, mark a characteristic moment in the literary development. Goldsmith's poems the *Traveller* (1765) and the *Deserted Village* (1770), and the *Vicar of Wakefield* (1766), are still on the old lines. The poetry adopts Pope's versification, and implies the same ideal; the desire for lucidity, sympathy, moderation, and the qualities which would generally be connoted by classical. The substance, distinguished from the style, shows the sympathy with sentimentalism of which Rousseau was to be the great exponent. Goldsmith is beginning to denounce luxury—a characteristic mark of the sentimentalist—and his regret for the period when 'every rood of earth maintained its man' is one side of the aspiration for a return to the state of nature and simplicity of manners. The inimitable Vicar recalls Sir Roger de Coverley and the gentle and delicate touch of Addison. But the Vicar is beginning to take an interest in philanthropy. He is impressed by the evils of the old prison system which had already roused Oglethorpe (who like Goldsmith—as I may notice—disputed with Johnson as to the evils of luxury) and was soon to arouse Howard. The greatest attraction of the Vicar is due to the personal charm of Goldsmith's character, but his character makes him sympathise with the wider social movements and the growth of genuine philanthropic sentiment. Goldsmith, in his remarks upon the *Present State of Polite Learning* (1759), explains the decay of literature (literature is always decaying) by the general enervation which accompanies learning and the want of originality caused by the growth of criticism. That was not an unnatural view at a time when the old forms are beginning to be inadequate for the new thoughts which are seeking for utterance. As yet, however, Goldsmith's own work proves sufficiently that the new motive could be so far adapted to the old form as to produce an artistic masterpiece. Sterne may illustrate a similar remark. He represents, no doubt, a kind of sham sentimentalism with an insincerity which has disgusted many able critics. He was resolved to attract notice at any price—by putting on cap and bells, and by the pruriency which stains his best work. Like many contemporaries he was reading old authors and turned them to account in a way which exposed him to the charge of plagiarism. He valued them for their quaintness. They enabled him to satisfy his propensity for being deliberately eccentric which made Horace Walpole call *Tristram Shandy* the 'dregs of nonsense,' and the learned Dr. Farmer prophesied that in twenty years it would be necessary to search antiquarian shops for a copy. Sterne's great achievement, however, was not in the mere buffoonery but in the passages where he continued the Addison tradition. Uncle Toby is a successor of Sir Roger, and the famous death of Lefevre is told with inimitable simplicity and delicacy of touch. Goldsmith and Sterne work upon the old lines, but make use of the new motives and materials which are beginning to interest readers, and which will in time call for different methods of treatment.

I must briefly indicate one other point. The society of which Garrick was a member, and which was both reading Shakespeare and seeing his plays revived, might well seem fitted to maintain a drama. Goldsmith complains of the decay of the stage, which he attributes partly to the exclusion of new pieces by the old Shakespearian drama. On that point he agrees as far as he dares with Voltaire. He ridiculed Home's *Douglas*, one of the last tragedies which made even a temporary success, and which certainly showed that the true impulse was extinct. But Goldsmith and his younger contemporary Sheridan succeeded for a time in restoring vigour to comedy. Their triumph over the sentimentalists Kelly and Cumberland showed, as Johnson put it, that they could fill the aim of the comedian, namely, making an audience merry. *She Stoops to Conquer* and *The School for Scandal* remain among genuine literary masterpieces. They are revivals of the old Congreve method, and imply the growth of a society more decent and free from the hard cynical brutality which disgraced the earlier writers. I certainly cannot give a sufficient reason why the society of Johnson and Reynolds, full of shrewd common sense, enjoying humour, and with a literary social tradition, should not have found other writers capable of holding up the comic mirror. I am upon the verge of a discussion which seems to be endless, the causes of the decay of the British stage. I must give it a wide berth, and only note that, as a fact, Sheridan took to politics, and his mantle fell on no worthy successor. The next craze (for which he was partly responsible) was the German theatre of Kotzebue, which represented the intrusion of new influences and the production of a great quantity of rubbish. After Goldsmith the poetic impulse seems to have decayed entirely. After the *Deserted Village* (1770) no striking work appeared till Crabbe published his first volume (1781), and was followed by his senior Cowper in 1782. Both of them employed the metre of Pope, though Cowper took to blank verse; and Crabbe, though he had read and admired Spenser, was to the end of his career a thorough disciple of Pope. Johnson read and revised his *Village*, which was thoroughly in harmony with the old gentleman's poetic creed. Yet both Cowper and Crabbe stimulate what may be called in some sense 'a return to nature'; though not in such a way as to announce a literary revolution. Each was restrained by personal conditions. Cowper's poetical aims were profoundly affected by his religious views. The movement which we call Methodist was essentially moral and philanthropic. It agreed so far with Rousseau's sentimentalism that it denounced the corruptions of the existing order; but instead of attributing the evils to the departure from the ideal state of nature, expressed them by the theological doctrine of the corruption of the human heart. That implied in some senses a fundamental difference. But there was a close coincidence in the judgment of actual motives. Cowper fully agreed with Rousseau that our rulers had become selfish and luxurious; that war was kept up to satisfy the ambition of kings and courtiers; that vice flourished because the aims of our rulers and teachers were low and selfish, and that slavery was a monstrous evil supported by the greed of traders. Brown's *Estimate*, he said, was thoroughly right as to our degeneracy, though Brown had not perceived the deepest root of the evil. Cowper's satire has lost its salt because he had retired too completely from the world to make a telling portrait. But he succeeds most admirably when he finds relief from the tortures of insanity by giving play to the exquisite playfulness and tenderness which was never destroyed by his melancholy. He delights us by an unconscious illustration of the simple domestic life in the quiet Olney fields, which we see in another form in the charming White of Selborne. He escapes from the ghastly images of religious insanity when he has indulged in the innocent play of tender and affectionate emotions, which finds itself revealed in tranquillising scenery. The literary result is a fresh appreciation of 'Nature.' Pope's Nature has become for him artificial and conventional. From a religious point of view it represents 'cold morality,' and the substitution of logical argumentation for the language of the heart. It suggests the cynicism of the heartless fine gentleman who sneers at Wesley and Bunyan, and covers his want of feeling by a stilted deism. Cowper tried unsuccessfully to supersede Pope's *Homer*; in trying to be simple he became bald; but he also tried most successfully to express with absolute sincerity the simple and deep emotions of an exquisitely tender character.

Crabbe meanwhile believed in Pope, and had a sturdy solid contempt for Methodism. Cowper's guide, Newton, would have passed with him for a nuisance and a fanatic. Crabbe is a thorough realist. In some ways he may be compared to his contemporary Malthus. Malthus started, as we know, by refuting the sentimentalism of Rousseau; Crabbe's *Village* is a protest against the embodiment of the same spirit in Goldsmith.

He is determined to see things as they are, with no rose-coloured mist. Crabbe replies to critics that if his realism was unpoetical, the criterion suggested would condemn much of Dryden and Pope as equally unpoetical. He was not renouncing but carrying on the tradition, and was admired by Byron in his rather wayward mood of Pope-worship as the last representative of the legitimate school. The position is significant. Crabbe condemns Goldsmith's 'Nature' because it is 'unnatural.' It means the Utopian ideal of Rousseau which never did and never can exist. It belongs to the world of old-fashioned pastoral poetry, in which Corydon and Thyrsis had their being. He will paint British squires and farmers and labourers as he has seen them with his own eyes. The wit has become for him the mere fop, whose poetry is an arbitrary convention, a mere plaything for the fine ladies and gentlemen detached from the living interests of mankind. The Pope tradition is still maintained, but is to be revised by being brought down again to contact with solid earth. Therefore on the one hand he is thoroughly in harmony with Johnson, the embodiment of common sense, and on the other, excited the enthusiasm of Wordsworth and

Scott, who, though leaders of a new movement, heartily sympathised with his realism and rejection of the old conventionalism. Though Crabbe regards Cowper's religion as fanaticism, they are so far agreed that both consider that poetry has become divorced from reality and reflects the ugly side of actual human nature. They do not propose a revolution in its methods, but to put fresh life into it by seeing things as they are. And both of them, living in the country, apply the principle to 'Nature' in the sense of scenery. Cowper gives interest to the flat meadows of the Ouse; and Crabbe, a botanist and lover of natural history, paints with unrivalled fidelity and force the flat shores and tideways of his native East Anglia. They are both therefore prophets of a love of Nature, in one of the senses of the Protean word. Cowper, who prophesied the fall of the Bastille and denounced luxury, was to some extent an unconscious ally of Rousseau, though he regarded the religious aspects of Rousseau's doctrine as shallow and unsatisfactory. Crabbe shows the attitude of which Johnson is the most characteristic example. Johnson was thoroughly content with the old school in so far as it meant that poetry must be thoroughly rational and sensible.

His hatred of cant and foppery was so far congenial to the tradition; but it implied a difference. To him Pope's metaphysical system was mere foppery, and the denunciation of luxury mere cant. He felt mere contempt for Goldsmith's flirtation with that vein of sentiment. His dogged conservatism prevented him from recognising the strength of the philosophical movements which were beginning to clothe themselves in Rousseauism. Burke, if he condemned the revolutionary doctrine as wicked, saw distinctly how potent a lesson it was becoming. Johnson, showing the true British indifference, could treat the movement with contempt—Hume's scepticism was a mere 'milking the bull'—a love of paradox for its own sake—and Wilkes and the Whigs, though wicked in intention, were simple and superficial dealers in big words. In the literary application the same sturdy common sense was opposed to the Pope tradition so far as that tradition opposed common sense. Conventional diction, pastorals, and twaddle about Nature belonged to the nonsensical side. He entirely sympathised with Crabbe's substitution of the real living brutish clown for the unreal swain of Arcadia; that is, for developing poetry by making it thoroughly realistic even at the cost of being prosaic.

So far the tendency to realism was thoroughly congenial to the matter-of-fact utilitarian spirit of the time, and was in some sense in harmony with a 'return to Nature.' But it was unconsciously becoming divorced from some of the great movements of thought, of which it failed to perceive the significance. A new inspiration was showing itself, to which critics have done at least ample justice. The growth of history had led to renewed interest in much that had been despised as mere curiosities or ridiculed as implying the barbarism of our ancestors. I have already noticed the dilettantism of the previous generation, and the interest of Gray and Collins and Warton and Walpole in antiquarian researches. Gothic had ceased to be a simple term of reproach. The old English literature is beginning to be studied seriously. Pope and Warburton and Johnson had all edited Shakespeare; Garrick had given him fresh popularity, and the first edition of *Old Plays* by Dodsley appeared in 1744. Similar studies were extending in many directions. Mallet in his work upon Denmark (1755) gave a translation of the *Eddas* which called attention to Scandinavian mythology. Bodmer soon afterwards published for the first time the *Nibelungen Lied*. Macpherson startled the literary world in 1762 by what professed to be an epic poem from the Gaelic. Chatterton's career (1752-1770) was a proof not only of unique poetical precocity, but of a singular facility in divining the tastes of the literary world at the time. Percy's *Reliques* appeared in 1765. Percy, I may note, had begun oddly enough by publishing a Chinese novel (1761), and a translation of Icelandic poetry (1763). Not long afterwards Sir William Jones published translations of Oriental poetry. Briefly, as historical, philological, and antiquarian research extended, the man of letters was also beginning to seek for new 'motives,' and to discover merits in old forms of literature. The importance of this new impulse cannot be over-estimated, but it may be partly misinterpreted. It is generally described as a foretaste of what is called the Romantic movement. The word is no doubt very useful—though exceedingly vague. The historian of literature is sometimes given to speak as though it meant the revelation of a new and definite creed. He speaks, that is, like the historian of science, who accepts Darwinism as the revelation of a new principle transfusing the old conceptions, and traces the various anticipations, the seminal idea; or like the Protestant theologian who used to regard Luther as having announced the full truth dimly foreseen by Wicliff or the Albigenses. Romanticism, that is, is treated as a single movement; while the men who share traces of the taste are supposed to have not only foreseen the new doctrine but to have been the actual originators. Yet I think that all competent writers will also agree that Romanticism is a name which has been applied to a number of divergent or inconsistent schools. It seems to mean every impulse which tended to find the old clothing inadequate for the new thoughts, which caused dissatisfaction with the old philosophical and religious or political systems and aspirations, and took a corresponding variety of literary forms. It is far too complex a phenomenon to be summed up in any particular formula. The mischief is that to take the literary evolution as an isolated phenomenon is to miss an essential clue to such continuity and unity as it really possesses. When we omit the social factor, the solidarity which exists between contemporaries occupied with the same problem and sharing certain common beliefs, each school appears as an independent unit, implying a discontinuity or a simple relation of contrariety, and we explain the succession by such a verbal phrase as 'reaction.' The real problem is, what does the reaction mean? and that requires us to take into account the complex and variously composed currents of thought and reason which are seeking for literary expression. The popularity of *Ossian* for example, is a curious phenomenon. At the first sight we are disposed to agree with Johnson that any man could write such stuff if he would abandon his mind to it, and to add that if any one would write it no one could read it. Yet we know that *Ossian* appealed to the gigantic intellects of Goethe and Napoleon. That is a symptom of deep significance; *Ossian* suited Goethe in the *Werther* period and Napoleon took it with him when he was dreaming of rivalling Alexander's conquests in the East. We may perhaps understand why the gigantesque pictures in *Ossian* of the northern mountains and scenery—with all its vagueness, incoherence, and bombast, was somehow congenial to minds dissatisfied, for different reasons, with the old ideals. To explain the charm more precisely is a very pretty problem for the acute critic. *Ossian*, it is clear, fell in with the mood characteristic of the time. But when we ask what effect it produced in English literature, the answer must surely be, 'next to none.' Gray was enthusiastic and tried to believe in its authenticity. Scots, like Blair and even the sceptical Hume—though Hume soon revolted—defended *Ossian* out of patriotic prejudice, and Burns professed to admire. But nobody in Great Britain took to writing Ossianesque. Wordsworth was simply disgusted by the unreality, and nothing could be less in the *Ossian* vein than Burns. The *Ossian* craze illustrates the extension of historical interest, of which I have spoken, and the vague discontent of Wertherism. But I do not see how the publication can be taken as the cause of a new departure, although it was an indication of the state of mind which led to a new departure. Percy's *Reliques*, again, is often mentioned as an 'epoch-making' book. Undoubtedly it was a favourite with Scott and many other readers of his generation. But how far did it create any change of taste? The old ballad was on one side congenial to the classical school, as Addison showed by his criticism of *Chevy Chase* for its simple version of a heroic theme. Goldsmith tried his hand at a ballad about the same time with Percy, and both showed that they were a little too much afraid that simplicity might degenerate into childishness, and gain Johnson's contempt. But there was nothing in the old school incompatible with a rather patronising appreciation of the popular poetry. It gained fresh interest when the historical tendency gave a newer meaning to the old society in which ballad poetry had flourished.

This suggests the last remark which I have room to make. One characteristic of the period is a growth of provincial centres of some intellectual culture. As manufactures extended, and manufacturers began to read, circles of some literary pretensions sprang up in Norwich, Birmingham, Bristol, and Manchester; and most conspicuously in Edinburgh. Though the Scot was coming south in numbers which alarmed Johnson, there were so many eminent Scots at home during this time that Edinburgh seems at least to have rivalled London as an intellectual centre. The list of great men includes Hume and Adam Smith, Robertson and Hailes and Adam Ferguson, Kames, Monboddo, and Dugald Stewart among philosophers and historians; John Home, Blair, G. Campbell, Beattie, and Henry Mackenzie among men of letters; Hutton, Black, Cullen, and Gregory among scientific leaders. Scottish patriotism then, as at other periods, was vigorous, and happily ceasing to be antagonistic to unionist sentiment. The Scot admitted that he was touched by provincialism; but he retained a national pride, and only made the modest and most justifiable claim that he was intrinsically superior to the Southron. He still preserved intellectual and social traditions, and cherished them the more warmly, which marked him as a distinct member of the United Kingdom. In Scotland the rapid industrial development had given fresh life to the whole society without obliterating its distinctive peculiarities. Song and ballad and local legends were still alive, and not merely objects of literary curiosity. It was under such conditions that Burns appeared, the greatest beyond compare of all the self-taught poets. Now there can be no explanation whatever of the occurrence of a man of genius at a given time and place. For anything we can say, Burns was an accident; but given the genius, his relation was clear, and the genius enabled him to recognise it with unequalled clearness. Burns became, as he has continued, the embodiment of the Scottish genius. Scottish patriotic feeling animates some of his noblest poems, and whether as an original writer—and no one could be more original—or as adapting and revising the existing poetry, he represents the essential spirit of the Scottish peasant. I need not point out that this implies certain limitations, and some failings worse than limitation. But it implies also the spontaneous and masculine vigour which we may call poetic inspiration of the highest kind. He had of course read the English authors such as Addison and Pope. So far as he tried to imitate the accepted form he was apt to lose his fire. He is inspired when he has a nation behind him and is the mouthpiece of sentiments, traditional, but also living and vigorous. He represents, therefore, a new period. The lyrical poetry seemed to have died out in England. It suddenly comes to life in Scotland and reaches unsurpassable excellence within certain limits, because a man of true genius rises to utter the emotions of a people in their most natural form without bothering about canons of literary criticism. The society and the individual are in thorough harmony, and that, I take it, is the condition of really great literature at all times.

This must suggest my concluding moral. The

watchword of every literary school may be brought under the formula 'Return to Nature': though 'Nature' receives different interpretations. To be natural, on the one hand, is to be sincere and spontaneous; to utter the emotions natural to you in the forms which are also natural, so far as the accepted canons are not rules imposed by authority but have been so thoroughly assimilated as to express your own instinctive impulses. On the other side, it means that the literature must be produced by the class which embodies the really vital and powerful currents of thought which are moulding society. The great author must have a people behind him; utter both what he really thinks and feels and what is thought and felt most profoundly by his contemporaries. As the literature ceases to be truly representative, and adheres to the conventionalism of the former period, it becomes 'unnatural' and the literary forms become a survival instead of a genuine creation. The history of eighteenth century literature illustrates this by showing how as the social changes give new influence to the middle classes and then to the democracy, the aristocratic class which represented the culture of the opening stage is gradually pushed aside; its methods become antiquated and its conventions cease to represent the ideals of the most vigorous part of the population. The return to Nature with Pope and Addison and Swift meant, get rid of pedantry, be thoroughly rational, and take for your guide the bright common sense of the Wit and the scholar. During Pope's supremacy the Wit who represents the aristocracy produces some admirably polished work ; but the development of journalism and Grub Street shows that he is writing to satisfy the popular interests so keenly watched by Defoe in Grub Street. In the period of Richardson and Fielding Nature has become the Nature of the middle-class John Bull. The old romances have become hopelessly unnatural, and they will give us portraits of living human beings, whether Clarissa or Tom Jones. The rationalism of the higher class strikes them as cynical, and the generation which listens to Wesley must have also a secular literature, which, whether sentimental as with Richardson or representing common sense with Fielding, must at any rate correspond to solid substantial matter-of-fact motives, intelligible to the ordinary Briton of the time. In the last period, the old literary conventions, though retaining their old literary prestige, are becoming threadbare while preserving the old forms. Even the Johnsonian conservatism implies hatred for cant, for mere foppery and sham sentimentalism; and though it uses them, insists with Crabbe upon keeping in contact with fact. We must be 'realistic,' though we can retain the old literary forms. The appeal to Nature, meanwhile, has come with Rousseau and the revolutionists to mean something different—the demand, briefly, for a thorough-going reconstruction of the whole philosophical and social fabric. To the good old Briton, Whig or Tory, that seemed to be either diabolical or mere Utopian folly. To him the British constitution is still thoroughly congenial and 'natural.' Meanwhile intellectual movement has introduced a new element. The historical sense is being developed, as a settled society with a complex organisation becomes conscious at once of its continuity and of the slow processes of growth by which it has been elaborated. The fusion of English and Scottish nations stimulates the patriotism of the smaller though better race, and generates a passionate enthusiasm for the old literature which represents the characteristic genius of the smaller community. Burns embodies the sentiment, though without any conscious reference to theories philosophical or historical. The significance was to be illustrated by Scott—an equally fervid patriot. He tells Crabbe how oddly a passage in the *Village* was associated in his memory with border-riding ballads and scraps of old plays. 'Nature' for Scott meant 'his honest grey hills' speaking in every fold of old traditional lore. That meant, in one sense, that Scott was not only romantic but reactionary. That was his weakness. But if he was the first to make the past alive, he was also the first to make the present historical. His masterpieces are not his descriptions of mediæval knights so much as the stories in which he illuminates the present by his vivid presentation of the present order as the outgrowth from the old, and makes the Scottish peasant or lawyer or laird interesting as a product and a type of social conditions. Nature therefore to him includes the natural processes by which society has been developed under the stress of circumstances. Nothing could be more unnatural for him than the revolutionary principle which despises tradition and regards the patriotic sentiment as superfluous and irrational. Wordsworth represents again another sense of Nature. He announced as his special principle that poetry should speak the language of Nature, and therefore, as he inferred, of the ordinary peasant and uneducated man. The hills did not speak to him of legend or history but of the sentiment of the unsophisticated yeoman or 'statesman.' He sympathised enthusiastically with the French Revolution so long as he took it to utter the simple republican sentiment congenial to a small society of farmers and shepherds. He abandoned it when he came to think that it really meant the dissolution of the religious and social sentiments which correspond to the deepest instincts which bound such men together. Coleridge represents a variation. He was the first Englishman to be affected by the philosophical movement of Germany. He had been an ardent revolutionist in the days when he adopted the metaphysics of Hartley and Priestley, which fell in with the main eighteenth-century current of scepticism. He came to think that the movement represented a perversion of the intellect. It meant materialism and scepticism, or interpreted Nature as a mere dead mechanism. It omitted, therefore, the essential element which is expressed by what we may roughly call the mystical tendency in philosophy. Nature must be taken as the embodiment of a divine idea. Nature, therefore, in his poetry, is regarded not from Scott's point of view as subordinate to human history, or from Wordsworth's as teaching the wisdom of unsophisticated mankind, but rather as a symbolism legible to the higher imagination. Though his fine critical sense made him keep his philosophy and his poetry distinct, that is the common tendency which gives unity to his work and which made his utterances so stimulating to congenial intellects. His criticism of the 'Nature' of Pope and Bolingbroke would be substantially, that in their hands the reason which professed to interpret Nature became cold and materialistic, because its logic left out of account the mysterious but essential touches revealed only to the heart, or, in his language, to the reason but not to the understanding. Meanwhile, though the French revolutionary doctrines were preached in England, they only attracted the literary leaders for a time, and it was not till the days of Byron and Shelley that they found thorough-going representatives in English poetry. On that, however, I must not speak. I have tried to indicate briefly how Scott and Wordsworth and Coleridge, the most eminent leaders of the new school, partly represented movements already obscurely working in England, and how they were affected by the new ideas which had sprung to life elsewhere. They, like their predecessors, are essentially trying to cast aside the literary 'survivals' of effete conditions, and succeed so far as they could find adequate expression for the great ideas of their time.

Printed by T. and A. Constable, Printers to His Majesty
at the Edinburgh University Press

Date Due

OCT 30 '64			
APR 22 '66			
FEB 15 1968			
MAR 18 1968			
MAY 1 '85			